PART 3

CERTIFICATION AND MAINTENANCE OF ISO 9001

Ensuring Long-term Compliance and Continuous Improvement for Small Enterprises

For All Business Sectors

DR. WILLIAM F. HARRINGTON

Certification and Maintenance of ISO 9001

Ensuring Long-term Compliance and Continuous Improvement for Small Enterprises

For All Business Sectors Part 3

Dr. William F. Harrington

DEDICATION

This book is dedicated to the countless small business owners, managers, and employees who continuously strive to improve their operations, enhance customer satisfaction, and build sustainable, quality-driven organizations.

To those who believe that every small step towards quality management leads to greater success, this guide is for you.

May this resource inspire your journey toward excellence.

Dr. William F. Harrington

Dr. William F. Harrington is a distinguished expert in ISO standards and operational excellence, with over 25 years of experience in guiding organizations through complex transformations and compliance initiatives. As the founder of Harrington Consulting, Dr. Harrington specializes in the implementation, auditing, and continuous improvement of ISO standards, including ISO 9001, ISO 27001, ISO 14001, and ISO 45001. His expertise enables businesses to streamline their processes, enhance compliance, and foster innovation through strategic alignment with internationally recognized standards.

In addition to his consulting work, Dr. Harrington is an accomplished educator and trainer, conducting customized ISO workshops for management teams and operational staff. His teaching focuses on equipping leaders with the knowledge and skills needed to effectively integrate ISO standards into their organizations.

Key Certifications:

Certification	Standard/Field
Certified Lead Auditor	ISO 9001 (Quality Management), ISO 27001 (Information Security), ISO 45001 (Occupational Health and Safety), ISO 14001 (Environmental Management), ISO 22301 (Business Continuity Management)
Certified Expert	ISO 31000 (Risk Management), ISO 50001 (Energy Management), ISO 37001 (Anti-corruption Management Systems)
Certified Trainer	Implementation and Auditing of ISO 9001, ISO 27001, ISO 14001, and ISO 45001

Notable Distinctions

Award	Description
ISO Excellence Award	For contributions to ISO certification
Global Leadership Award	Awarded by the International Organization for Standardization (ISO)
Top 50 Global ISO Experts	For leadership in ISO standards

Academy IQC Vienna

Welcome to Academy IQC Vienna — your hub for innovative online learning and resources to boost quality management, ISO 9001:2015 compliance, and business performance through tailored courses, e-forms, and coaching.

Service	Description	Link
E-Workshop	Join interactive e-workshops that provide in-depth training on **ISO standards**, **quality management**, and **risk management**. Engage in practical exercises.	https://academy.iqc-vienna.com/e-workshop/
E-Coaching	Get personalized coaching from industry experts. Whether you need guidance on **ISO certification**, **audit preparation**, or process optimization.	https://academy.iqc-vienna.com/e-coaching/
Online Courses	Take advantage of our self-paced online courses designed to help you master **ISO standards**, enhance **quality management**, and develop necessary skills.	https://academy.iqc-vienna.com/online-courses/
Documentation Kits	Streamline your **ISO 9001** implementation with comprehensive documentation kits, including templates for **policies**, **procedures**, and **forms**.	https://academy.iqc-vienna.com/documentation-kits/

Special Offer

INTRODUCTION

Achieving **ISO 9001 certification** is a significant milestone for any small enterprise. It demonstrates a commitment to maintaining quality standards, improving operational efficiency, and meeting customer expectations. However, the journey doesn't end once certification is achieved. Maintaining ISO 9001 compliance and continuously improving your Quality Management System (QMS) is equally crucial for long-term success.

This book provides a comprehensive guide on **ISO 9001 certification**, the process of **maintaining compliance**, and the steps involved in ensuring that your QMS evolves with the organization's growth and changing market demands. Whether you're preparing for an initial certification or seeking to renew or upgrade your existing certification, this book will serve as an invaluable resource.

BENEFITS OF ISO 9001 CERTIFICATION

ISO 9001 certification offers several key benefits for small enterprises, helping them improve their processes, enhance customer satisfaction, and increase their market competitiveness.

1. **Improved Customer Satisfaction**:

   Certification ensures that your products or services consistently meet customer expectations, leading to higher customer satisfaction and loyalty.

2. **Operational Efficiency**:

   The implementation of ISO 9001 leads to more **efficient processes** by standardizing procedures, reducing waste, and enhancing productivity.

3. **Better Decision-Making**:

   With clear data and regular performance reviews, ISO 9001 helps organizations make informed decisions based on reliable, measurable metrics.

4. **Market Competitiveness**:

ISO 9001 certification is recognized globally. It positions your company as a reliable and **high-quality provider**, helping you gain a competitive edge in your industry.

5. **Continuous Improvement**:

   ISO 9001 is not a one-time effort. The standard promotes ongoing evaluation and improvements, helping your organization adapt to changes and drive long-term success.

6. **Improved Employee Engagement**:

   By involving employees in quality initiatives, ISO 9001 fosters a sense of ownership and responsibility, leading to better engagement and morale.

WHY CHOOSE ISO 9001 FOR YOUR SMALL ENTERPRISE?

ISO 9001 is the most widely recognized **Quality Management System (QMS)** standard in the world. For small enterprises, the **cost-effective** nature of the standard makes it an ideal framework for improving processes, ensuring quality, and gaining trust in the marketplace. Here are several reasons why small businesses should choose ISO 9001:

1. **Boosts Credibility and Reputation**:

   ISO 9001 certification gives your business credibility, especially when dealing with large customers, government agencies, or international partners. It assures them that you meet internationally recognized quality standards.

2. **Affordable and Scalable**:

   ISO 9001 can be adapted to businesses of all sizes. Its flexibility allows small enterprises to implement a QMS that suits their specific needs without unnecessary complexity.

3. **Helps with Regulatory Compliance**:

Many industries require specific standards for compliance. ISO 9001 helps small businesses stay in line with **regulatory** and **legal requirements**, reducing the risk of compliance issues.

4. **Strengthens Supplier Relationships**:

   ISO 9001 certification often opens up new opportunities with suppliers. It demonstrates your commitment to quality and your ability to manage supplier relationships effectively.

5. **Prepares for Future Growth**:

   Implementing ISO 9001 now helps prepare your business for future expansion. It ensures your processes are scalable and that quality is embedded in every aspect of the business.

WHO SHOULD CHOOSE ISO 9001 CERTIFICATION?

ISO 9001 certification is suitable for businesses of all sizes, but small enterprises particularly benefit due to the standard's scalability and flexibility. Small businesses can use ISO 9001 to lay a strong foundation for growth, improve internal processes, and enhance customer satisfaction.

Key stakeholders who can benefit from ISO 9001 certification include:

1. **Small Business Owners**:

   Small business owners who want to improve their business processes, increase efficiency, and establish credibility in the market will find ISO 9001 a valuable tool.

2. **Quality Managers**:

   Quality managers in small enterprises can use ISO 9001 as a structured framework to implement and maintain quality management practices, ensuring compliance and continual improvement.

3. **Operations Managers**:

Operations managers can apply ISO 9001 to streamline processes, reduce waste, and improve operational efficiency, leading to better overall performance.

4. **Suppliers and Vendors**:

   Small businesses that rely on suppliers and vendors can use ISO 9001 to strengthen relationships and ensure that external providers meet quality standards.

5. **Exporting Companies**:

   Small enterprises that plan to expand internationally or want to enter new markets will find ISO 9001 a critical asset for gaining global recognition and compliance with international standards.

This book will guide you through the essential steps of achieving ISO 9001 certification, maintaining it, and ensuring that your QMS continues to improve over time. Whether you are starting the certification process or looking to improve an existing system, you will find valuable insights and practical advice to help you succeed.

Table of Contents

CHAPTER I

Introduction to ISO 9001 for Small Enterprises

WHAT IS ISO 9001?

ISO 9001 is the most widely recognized and globally adopted standard for **Quality Management Systems (QMS)**. It provides a structured approach to ensuring that an organization consistently meets customer requirements and delivers high-quality products or services. The **ISO 9001:2015** standard focuses on improving operational efficiency, ensuring customer satisfaction, and providing a framework for continual improvement in all aspects of an organization's operations.

ISO 9001 is applicable to **organizations of all sizes** and industries, including small enterprises, and provides clear guidelines for implementing a QMS that ensures compliance with both customer and regulatory requirements. While the standard originated in the manufacturing industry, it is now applicable across all sectors, including **services**, **construction**, **healthcare**, and **education**.

Key Principles of ISO 9001

ISO 9001 is based on several **key principles** that organizations should adopt to ensure their QMS is effective and aligned with business goals. These principles serve as a guide to improve the efficiency, quality, and sustainability of an organization. The seven principles of ISO 9001 are:

1. **Customer Focus**:

   The primary focus of ISO 9001 is on meeting customer requirements and exceeding customer expectations. Organizations must understand customer needs and continuously strive to improve satisfaction.

2. **Leadership**:

Effective leadership is essential for the success of a QMS. Leaders must establish a vision, set objectives, and create an environment where employees can contribute to achieving the organization's goals.

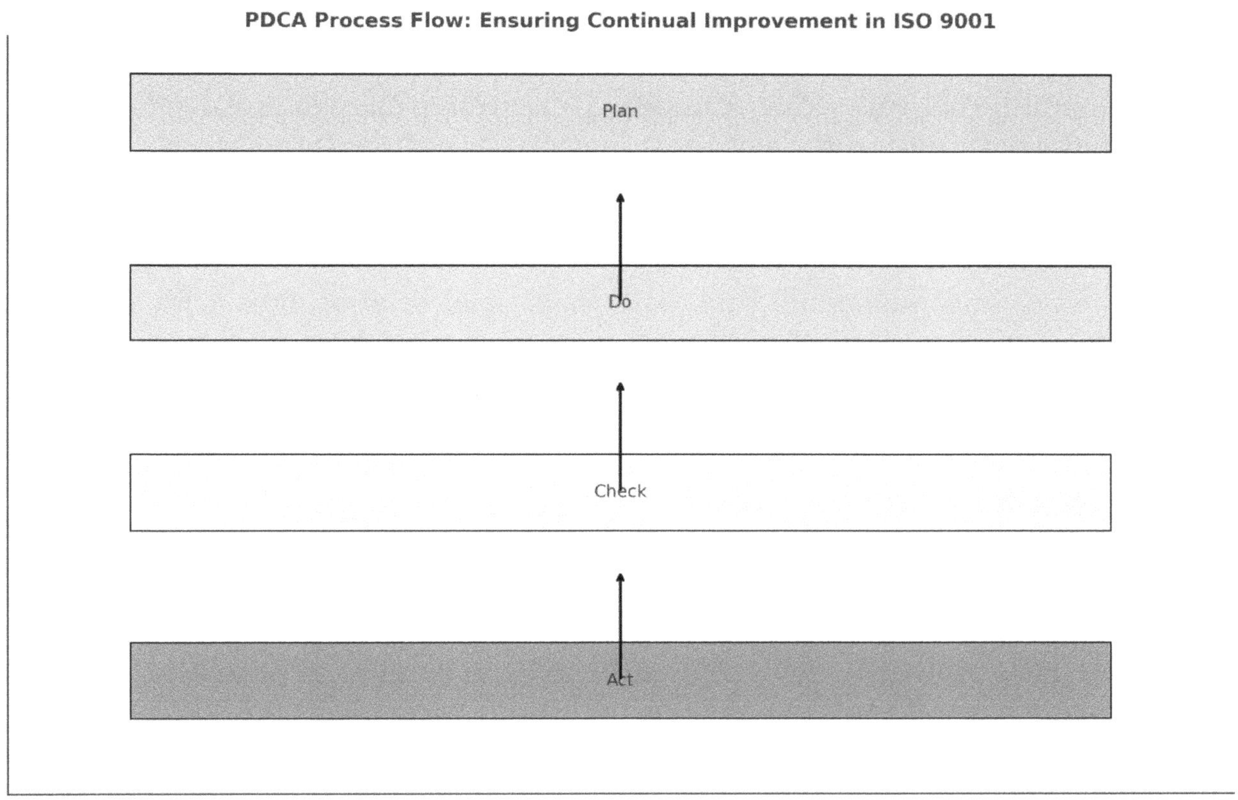

3. **Engagement of People**:

   Engaging employees at all levels ensures that everyone contributes to the QMS. It promotes a culture of responsibility, involvement, and continuous improvement.

4. **Process Approach**:

   ISO 9001 encourages organizations to view their activities as a series of interrelated processes that work together to achieve common objectives. This ensures efficiency and helps reduce waste and defects.

5. **Improvement**:

A QMS must focus on continual improvement. Organizations are encouraged to continually evaluate and enhance their processes to maintain and improve their ability to meet customer expectations.

6. **Evidence-based Decision Making**:

   Decisions should be based on **data** and **factual evidence** rather than assumptions or subjective opinions. This ensures that the organization makes informed, objective decisions that improve overall performance.

7. **Relationship Management**:

   Building and maintaining mutually beneficial relationships with suppliers, partners, and other stakeholders is vital. Strong relationships contribute to sustained success by ensuring the quality and reliability of products and services.

Why Is ISO 9001 Important for Small Enterprises?

For small enterprises, adopting ISO 9001 can significantly improve internal processes and help compete effectively in the marketplace. While many small businesses may initially view ISO 9001 as a complex or resource-intensive certification, the benefits often outweigh the costs, especially as the business grows. Here are some reasons why ISO 9001 is essential for small enterprises:

1. **Improved Process Efficiency**:

   ISO 9001 helps small businesses streamline their operations, eliminate waste, and reduce errors, leading to higher efficiency and lower operational costs.

2. **Enhanced Customer Satisfaction**:

   By focusing on meeting customer requirements and delivering high-quality products or services, small businesses can improve customer satisfaction, leading to increased loyalty and repeat business.

3. **Better Risk Management**:

ISO 9001 encourages organizations to identify potential risks and implement controls to mitigate them, reducing the likelihood of failures, complaints, and operational disruptions.

4. **Access to New Markets**:

   ISO 9001 certification is recognized globally and can help small businesses gain entry into new markets, including partnerships with larger organizations or international trade.

5. **Improved Employee Engagement**:

   By involving employees in the QMS, ISO 9001 fosters a sense of responsibility, teamwork, and pride in achieving quality goals, leading to increased motivation and job satisfaction.

6. **Compliance with Regulations**:

   ISO 9001 helps small businesses stay compliant with industry regulations and customer expectations, reducing the risk of non-compliance penalties and enhancing the organization's reputation.

7. **Continuous Improvement Culture**:

   ISO 9001 instills a culture of continuous improvement, where the business is always looking for ways to optimize processes, reduce defects, and innovate.

How Does ISO 9001 Work?

ISO 9001 operates through the **Plan-Do-Check-Act (PDCA)** cycle, which is a framework for improving processes and ensuring that objectives are met. The PDCA cycle is a continuous loop, ensuring that the organization constantly reviews and enhances its quality management practices.

1. **Plan**:
   Establish the goals, objectives, and processes required to meet customer requirements and improve overall performance.

2. **Do**:
   Implement the processes and procedures that support the achievement of the planned objectives.
3. **Check**:
   Monitor and measure performance to ensure that the processes are working as intended.
4. **Act**:
   Take corrective actions when necessary to address any issues or opportunities for improvement.

This iterative process drives continuous improvement and allows small businesses to adapt quickly to changing customer needs, market conditions, or operational challenges.

Implementation of ISO 9001 in Small Enterprises

Implementing ISO 9001 in a small enterprise requires a step-by-step approach to ensure that the QMS is correctly established and maintained. The process involves:

1. **Commitment from Management**:

   Leadership must be fully committed to the ISO 9001 implementation process. This includes setting the vision, objectives, and allocating resources.

2. **Employee Involvement**:

   Employees must be engaged in the QMS to ensure that they understand their role in quality management and are motivated to contribute to the improvement of processes.

3. **Defining Processes**:

   Identify key processes that impact quality and customer satisfaction. Establish clear procedures and responsibilities to ensure consistency.

4. **Documentation and Record Keeping**:

Proper documentation is essential for ensuring that processes are standardized and easily reviewed. This includes creating a **Quality Manual**, **procedures**, and **work instructions**.

5. **Monitoring and Measurement**:

   Establish a system for measuring process performance and customer satisfaction. Regular audits, feedback, and reviews help identify areas for improvement.

6. **Continuous Improvement**:

   Ensure that improvement is ongoing by setting objectives, analyzing data, and taking corrective actions when necessary.

Conclusion

ISO 9001 provides a comprehensive framework for small enterprises to enhance quality, improve efficiency, and increase customer satisfaction. It helps organizations achieve consistency in their operations, mitigate risks, and foster a culture of **continual improvement**. The standard's focus on **process management**, **customer focus**, and **leadership** ensures that organizations stay competitive, compliant, and responsive to customer needs.

Implementing ISO 9001 may seem like a challenging task, but with a structured approach and commitment from management, small businesses can enjoy long-term benefits, including increased operational efficiency, improved customer relationships, and a stronger market position.

Benefits of ISO 9001 for Small Enterprises

ISO 9001:2015 provides a structured framework for organizations to consistently meet customer requirements and enhance overall operational performance. While this internationally recognized standard is applicable to businesses of all sizes, it brings unique advantages to **small enterprises**. By adopting ISO 9001, small businesses can streamline processes, improve customer satisfaction, and position themselves for growth and sustainability in a competitive marketplace.

Below are the primary benefits that small enterprises can gain from **ISO 9001 certification**:

1. Improved Customer Satisfaction

One of the core principles of ISO 9001 is customer focus. The standard emphasizes the need for businesses to understand their customers' needs and consistently meet their expectations. Small enterprises that implement ISO 9001 are better equipped to address customer concerns promptly, ensuring high levels of satisfaction. By maintaining a focus on customer needs, businesses can build strong relationships, encourage loyalty, and generate positive word-of-mouth referrals.

2. Enhanced Operational Efficiency

ISO 9001 provides a clear set of processes and guidelines for organizations to follow. By standardizing procedures and aligning operations with quality management principles, small enterprises can significantly reduce inefficiencies and waste. This leads to better use of resources, faster turnaround times, and improved productivity, which ultimately translates into lower costs and higher profit margins.

3. Better Decision Making

ISO 9001 promotes evidence-based decision-making, which means that business decisions should be based on reliable data rather than assumptions or subjective opinions. By adopting this approach, small businesses can make more informed decisions that are in the best interest of the company, its employees, and customers. Regular performance reviews, audits, and feedback mechanisms provide valuable data that can guide decision-making processes.

4. Increased Competitiveness and Market Access

ISO 9001 certification is a mark of quality that is recognized globally. For small enterprises looking to expand their market share or enter new markets, ISO 9001 certification provides a competitive edge. Many customers, particularly in industries like manufacturing, supply chain, or government contracting, require ISO 9001 certification from their suppliers. By being ISO certified, small businesses can gain access to more opportunities, including partnerships with larger organizations and international clients.

5. Continual Improvement Culture

One of the hallmarks of ISO 9001 is its focus on continual improvement. ISO 9001 encourages businesses to regularly assess their processes, identify areas for improvement, and make necessary adjustments. For small businesses, this philosophy can drive innovation, lead to better customer service, and help ensure long-term sustainability. Small enterprises can also quickly adapt to changes in customer demands, industry trends, or regulations, staying competitive in a dynamic market.

6. Risk Management

ISO 9001 requires organizations to identify potential risks to quality and implement strategies to mitigate them. By adopting a proactive approach to risk management, small enterprises can avoid costly disruptions, product defects, or compliance issues. Regular risk assessments help businesses anticipate challenges and put preventative measures in place, reducing the likelihood of costly mistakes or nonconformities.

7. Employee Engagement and Satisfaction

Engaged employees are vital to the success of any business. ISO 9001 involves employees at all levels in quality management and process improvement, fostering a sense of ownership and responsibility. Employees who are part of a structured system with clear objectives and quality standards tend to be more motivated, productive, and committed to the company's success. This leads to higher job satisfaction, reduced turnover, and a positive work environment.

Table: Summary of Benefits for Small Enterprises Implementing ISO 9001

Benefit	Description	Impact on Small Enterprise
Improved Customer Satisfaction	Ensures products and services consistently meet customer needs and expectations.	Increased customer loyalty, positive feedback, and more referrals.
Enhanced Operational Efficiency	Streamlines processes, reduces waste, and improves productivity.	Lower operational costs and improved profitability.
Better Decision Making	Decisions based on objective data and reliable performance metrics.	More informed and accurate business decisions, reducing errors.
Increased Competitiveness	Positions the business as a credible and reliable supplier through ISO 9001 certification.	Opens new market opportunities, especially with large clients or international markets.

Continual Improvement Culture	Focuses on constantly refining processes and practices to better meet customer and business needs.	Drives innovation and adaptability to changing market conditions.
Risk Management	Identifies potential risks and establishes measures to prevent issues.	Reduces operational disruptions and nonconformities, ensuring smoother operations.
Employee Engagement	Involves employees in the quality management system, enhancing their role in process improvements.	Increased employee motivation, satisfaction, and retention.

Conclusion

For small enterprises, adopting ISO 9001:2015 can significantly improve their **quality management processes**, resulting in higher customer satisfaction, better operational efficiency, and greater competitiveness. The benefits of **standardized processes**, **data-driven decision making**, and a **culture of continual improvement** can propel small businesses toward long-term success.

By implementing ISO 9001, small businesses not only improve their internal processes but also enhance their reputation and market position, paving the way for sustainable growth and a loyal customer base.

Key Principles of Quality Management

Quality management is the foundation of any successful **Quality Management System (QMS)**, and in the context of **ISO 9001:2015**, the standard is built upon **seven core principles**. These principles guide organizations in developing an effective QMS that focuses on continuous improvement, customer satisfaction, and operational excellence.

Here are the **seven key principles of quality management**:

1. Customer Focus

The **customer focus** principle emphasizes that an organization should **understand and meet customer needs**. This includes ensuring that products and services are designed, developed, and delivered to meet or exceed customer expectations.

Businesses must recognize the importance of customer feedback and use it as a source of continuous improvement.

- **Key Actions**:
  - Identify customer needs and expectations.
  - Measure customer satisfaction regularly.
  - Build strong customer relationships to enhance loyalty.
  - Proactively address customer concerns and complaints.
- **Benefit**:
  Improving customer satisfaction directly leads to increased loyalty, repeat business, and referrals, which are critical for long-term success.

2. Leadership

Leadership refers to the commitment of top management to guide the organization toward achieving its quality objectives. Effective leadership establishes a clear vision, fosters an environment where employees can engage, and provides direction for the QMS.

- **Key Actions**:
  - Top management should set clear goals and objectives.
  - Leaders must provide resources and support for quality initiatives.
  - Promote a culture where employees are empowered to make decisions related to quality.
- **Benefit**:
  Strong leadership drives alignment within the organization, motivating employees to work towards common goals and ensuring the success of the QMS.

3. Engagement of People

This principle emphasizes the importance of involving **employees at all levels** in the quality management process. Engaging people ensures that everyone contributes to achieving the organization's quality goals and that quality becomes part of the organization's culture.

- **Key Actions**:
  - Involve employees in decision-making and problem-solving.
  - Provide training and development opportunities.
  - Recognize and reward contributions to quality improvement.

- **Benefit**:
  Engaged employees are more likely to be motivated, productive, and committed to improving quality standards. This leads to better performance and a more positive organizational culture.

4. Process Approach

The **process approach** involves managing interrelated processes as a system to achieve more consistent and predictable results. By understanding and managing processes, organizations can improve efficiency, reduce errors, and better control their operations.

- **Key Actions**:
  - Identify key processes and how they interact.
  - Optimize and standardize processes for better results.
  - Monitor and evaluate process performance regularly.
- **Benefit**:
  A process approach ensures that resources are used efficiently, waste is minimized, and processes consistently deliver the intended outcomes.

5. Improvement

The **improvement** principle focuses on the need for continual enhancement in the organization's processes, products, services, and the QMS itself. ISO 9001 encourages organizations to embrace a culture of **continuous improvement** to achieve higher levels of performance.

- **Key Actions**:
  - Set improvement goals and identify opportunities for optimization.
  - Implement corrective and preventive actions based on data analysis.
  - Foster an environment where innovation and creativity are encouraged.
- **Benefit**:
  Continuous improvement ensures that the organization remains adaptable, innovative, and competitive. It helps the organization evolve to meet changing customer needs and market conditions.

6. Evidence-Based Decision Making

Evidence-based decision making means that decisions should be based on **data and facts**, rather than assumptions or gut feelings. Organizations should use accurate, reliable data to evaluate performance, identify issues, and make decisions that lead to effective outcomes.

- **Key Actions**:
  - Collect relevant data through audits, surveys, and performance metrics.
  - Analyze data to identify trends, root causes of issues, and opportunities for improvement.
  - Make informed decisions that are based on facts and objective evidence.
- **Benefit**:
  Using data to guide decisions increases the likelihood of making successful, effective choices that positively impact performance, compliance, and customer satisfaction.

7. Relationship Management

Relationship management refers to the need for organizations to manage their relationships with all stakeholders, including suppliers, customers, partners, and employees. Strong relationships create value for all parties involved and contribute to long-term success.

- **Key Actions**:
  - Build mutually beneficial relationships with suppliers and external partners.
  - Collaborate with stakeholders to enhance product and service offerings.
  - Communicate openly and regularly with all stakeholders to align objectives.
- **Benefit**:
  Effective relationship management leads to better cooperation, more reliable partnerships, and increased value from suppliers and stakeholders, which ultimately supports organizational growth and stability.

Table: Overview of the Seven Principles of Quality Management

Principle	Description	Key Actions	Benefit

Customer Focus	Understanding and meeting customer needs and expectations.	Identify needs, measure satisfaction, address concerns.	Increased loyalty, repeat business, referrals.
Leadership	Guiding the organization with a clear vision and strong direction.	Set goals, provide resources, support quality initiatives.	Alignment within the organization, motivated employees.
Engagement of People	Involving employees in the QMS process to foster ownership and accountability.	Involve employees in decision-making, provide training and rewards.	Improved motivation, performance, and job satisfaction.
Process Approach	Managing interrelated processes as a system to improve efficiency.	Identify and optimize key processes, monitor performance.	Reduced errors, better resource utilization.
Improvement	Continuously enhancing processes, products, and services.	Set improvement goals, implement corrective and preventive actions.	Long-term innovation and competitiveness.
Evidence-Based Decision Making	Making decisions based on accurate, reliable data.	Collect data, analyze performance, make informed decisions.	More effective decisions and outcomes.
Relationship Management	Managing relationships with stakeholders for mutual benefit.	Build partnerships, communicate openly, collaborate with suppliers.	Stronger partnerships, increased value.

Conclusion

The **seven principles of quality management** form the foundation of **ISO 9001:2015** and guide organizations toward achieving a high level of performance and customer satisfaction. By applying these principles, organizations can build a **robust Quality Management System (QMS)** that ensures continual improvement, fosters employee engagement, and strengthens relationships with customers and suppliers.

Adopting these principles helps organizations stay competitive, adapt to changes, and deliver consistent value to customers and other stakeholders, ensuring long-term success and growth.

CHAPTER 2

Achieving and Maintaining ISO 9001 Certification

This chapter focuses on the critical aspects of achieving **ISO 9001 certification** and maintaining it over time, ensuring that the **Quality Management System (QMS)** remains aligned with the organization's evolving business needs, market demands, and customer expectations. It goes beyond just achieving certification; the goal is to ensure the QMS is sustainable, adaptable, and continuously improves to support long-term success.

1. Building a Robust ISO 9001 Framework for Long-Term Success

A successful **ISO 9001 implementation** is not a one-time event but rather an ongoing journey. Organizations must focus on embedding the QMS into the core structure and culture of the business. Achieving and maintaining certification requires a framework that is not only compliant with ISO 9001 standards but also capable of evolving as the organization grows and faces new challenges.

Integrating ISO 9001 with Organizational Culture

For ISO 9001 to be effective in the long term, it must become an integral part of the organization's **culture**. This means that quality management should not be seen as a separate or external requirement but as a core value that permeates every level of the organization. Achieving this requires commitment from top management, clear communication of quality goals, and active engagement from all employees.

- **Leadership Commitment**: Top management must champion the QMS and demonstrate leadership by embedding quality principles into the organizational culture. This commitment is key to making the QMS sustainable and meaningful.
- **Employee Involvement**: Quality must be seen as everyone's responsibility. When employees at all levels are engaged in maintaining quality standards,

the system becomes ingrained in the company's daily operations and decision-making processes.

- **Continuous Improvement**: ISO 9001's focus on **continuous improvement** means that the organization must adapt to changes in the market and internal business conditions. A culture that embraces continuous improvement helps ensure that the QMS evolves to meet the organization's changing needs.

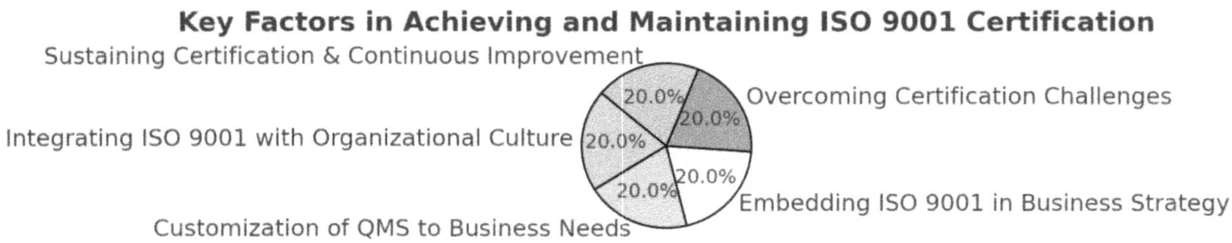

Customization of the QMS to Evolving Business Needs

One of the strengths of ISO 9001 is its **flexibility**. The standard is designed to be adaptable to different industries, sizes, and types of organizations. As businesses evolve, their QMS needs to evolve too. This requires customizing the QMS to reflect the organization's specific context, including industry requirements, market dynamics, and business size.

- **Tailoring for Organizational Size and Complexity**: Smaller businesses may need a simplified QMS with fewer formal processes, while larger businesses may require more robust systems with more complex documentation and reporting. The QMS must grow with the organization and adapt to changes in structure and market demands.
- **Industry-Specific Adaptations**: Different industries have unique challenges and regulatory requirements. The QMS must be customized to ensure it addresses industry-specific quality standards, whether it's manufacturing, healthcare, education, or services.
- **Market Needs**: As market conditions change, the QMS should be able to adapt. For example, increasing customer expectations for faster delivery times or more environmentally friendly products may require adjustments in quality processes to meet these demands.

Embedding ISO 9001 in Business Strategy

ISO 9001 should not exist in isolation. To create a **robust** and **sustainable** QMS, it must be fully integrated into the organization's **business strategy**. This ensures that the QMS supports the organization's overall goals and helps drive business success.

- **Aligning Quality with Business Goals**: The QMS should support strategic objectives, such as improving customer satisfaction, increasing operational efficiency, reducing costs, or expanding market share. By aligning quality goals with business goals, the organization ensures that the QMS is not just about compliance, but about contributing to long-term growth and competitiveness.
- **Quality as a Strategic Asset**: Quality is no longer just about meeting the minimum standards—it's a strategic asset that can differentiate an organization from its competitors. A well-aligned QMS helps an organization continuously meet or exceed customer expectations, leading to improved customer loyalty and increased market share.
- **Regular Strategy Reviews**: The alignment of the QMS with business strategy requires periodic reviews. The organization must regularly assess whether its quality objectives and processes are still in line with its changing strategic goals and market demands.

2. Overcoming Certification Challenges

Achieving ISO 9001 certification can be challenging, and maintaining certification requires consistent effort and focus. This section would address common obstacles organizations face during both the **initial certification** and the **maintenance phases**.

Handling Common Certification Challenges

- **Resistance to Change**: Many employees may resist the changes that come with ISO 9001 implementation, especially if the QMS significantly alters how they work. Overcoming this resistance requires clear communication, involving employees in the process, and providing necessary training.
- **Resource Constraints**: Smaller enterprises often face **resource constraints**, making it difficult to allocate enough time and budget for the certification process. Effective planning, prioritization, and support from top management are essential to overcome this.

- **Balancing Certification with Business Operations**: The implementation of ISO 9001 can sometimes disrupt day-to-day operations, especially when significant changes are required. Managing this balance is critical to ensure that certification doesn't negatively affect business productivity.

Sustaining Certification and Continuous Improvement

Once certification is achieved, it is important to ensure the QMS continues to operate effectively and improve over time.

- **Ongoing Internal Audits and Reviews**: Regular internal audits ensure that the QMS is still compliant with ISO 9001 and remains aligned with organizational goals. Audits also provide an opportunity to identify areas for improvement and take corrective actions.
- **Management Reviews**: Top management must regularly review the performance of the QMS to ensure it remains relevant and effective. Reviews should focus on customer feedback, audit results, and any external or internal changes that might affect quality objectives.
- **Employee Training and Engagement**: Ongoing training is necessary to ensure that employees understand the evolving quality standards and the organization's goals. Keeping the workforce engaged with the QMS is vital for sustaining certification.

3. Overcoming Post-Certification Challenges

Achieving ISO 9001 certification is just the beginning. Organizations must also face challenges in maintaining their certification over time. Post-certification challenges can include adapting to changing business environments, customer expectations, and regulatory requirements.

- **Responding to Audit Findings**: After certification, the organization must address any **nonconformities** or areas for improvement identified during internal or external audits. Effective corrective actions are necessary to ensure compliance and continuous improvement.
- **Maintaining Consistency in Processes**: As the organization grows, maintaining consistent processes across departments and locations can become challenging. The QMS must evolve and adapt to these changes while still ensuring that quality standards are maintained.
- **Managing Employee Turnover**: Changes in staff, particularly in key roles like quality management or senior leadership, can disrupt the QMS. Ensuring

continuity through proper documentation and knowledge transfer is essential to maintaining the QMS.

Conclusion

Achieving and maintaining **ISO 9001 certification** requires a structured approach that not only focuses on meeting the certification requirements but also integrates quality management into the organization's **core operations**. By aligning the **QMS** with business objectives, continuously improving processes, and overcoming challenges, organizations can ensure the long-term sustainability of their ISO 9001 certification and continue to meet the expectations of customers, stakeholders, and regulatory bodies.

2. Challenges and Solutions in Maintaining ISO 9001 Certification

ISO 9001 certification is not a one-time achievement but a continual process of improvement and adaptation. While it provides organizations with a structured framework for quality management, maintaining this certification comes with a set of challenges. In this section, we will explore common obstacles faced by organizations post-certification and provide strategies for overcoming them.

Dealing with Certification Fatigue

After achieving ISO 9001 certification, organizations may experience **certification fatigue**, where employees feel disengaged, or overwhelmed, especially during periodic audits or when working towards continual improvements.

- **Proactive Engagement**: To prevent burnout, it's essential to maintain high levels of **employee engagement** and **motivation** throughout the implementation and maintenance phases. Regular communication about the value of the QMS, positive reinforcement, and recognizing team efforts help prevent disengagement.
- **Efficient Use of Resources**: Avoid overburdening staff by scheduling audits and reviews during less busy periods. Consider using **internal resources** for certain tasks instead of relying on external consultants to save time and reduce stress.

Challenge	Solution
Certification Fatigue	Engage employees proactively and avoid overwhelming them during audits.

Overwhelming Workloads	Ensure proper planning of resources, including time management and staff schedules.

Addressing Changing Market Demands

As businesses grow and market conditions evolve, so too must the QMS. Ensuring that **ISO 9001 remains relevant** involves adapting the system to **technological shifts**, **changing customer expectations**, and **regulatory updates**.

- **Technological Adaptation**: Keep the QMS flexible enough to incorporate new technologies that may affect business operations. For instance, integrating **automation**, **AI tools**, or **digital platforms** into the QMS can improve processes and ensure compliance.
- **Customer-Centric Approach**: Regularly gather customer feedback and incorporate it into the QMS to align quality objectives with customer expectations. This can be done through customer surveys, satisfaction ratings, and performance reviews.

Challenge	Solution
Changing Market Needs	Continuously monitor market trends and adjust the QMS to meet evolving customer expectations.
Technological Changes	Integrate new technologies and digital solutions into the QMS for efficiency and innovation.

Mitigating Compliance Drift

Over time, organizations may experience **compliance drift**, where their adherence to ISO 9001 standards diminishes, often due to lack of attention or inconsistent internal audits.

- **Self-Assessments**: Regular self-assessments help identify areas where compliance may be slipping. These can be conducted through internal audits, management reviews, and feedback loops from employees and customers.
- **Gap Analysis**: Performing gap analysis helps uncover discrepancies between the current QMS and the ISO 9001 requirements, allowing the organization to take corrective action before non-compliance occurs.

Challenge	Solution
Compliance Drift	Perform regular self-assessments and gap analysis to ensure compliance.

3. Strategies for Continuous Improvement Beyond Certification

ISO 9001 certification is just the beginning of a continuous journey. This section discusses strategies for building a culture of continuous improvement and sustaining ISO 9001 certification over the long term.

Building a Systematic Culture of Continuous Improvement

A culture of **continuous improvement** (CI) is central to the success of ISO 9001. This involves systematically identifying, addressing, and tracking improvement opportunities across all business functions.

- **Data-Driven Decisions**: Leveraging **data analytics** can help identify areas of inefficiency and process bottlenecks. By analyzing performance metrics, organizations can make informed decisions about process improvements.
- **Employee Feedback**: Employees play a critical role in identifying areas for improvement. Encouraging them to submit feedback, participate in brainstorming sessions, and be part of the problem-solving process enhances engagement and leads to more effective solutions.

Strategy	Description
Data Analytics	Use data to identify inefficiencies and improve processes.
Employee Feedback	Encourage staff involvement in continuous improvement initiatives.

Leveraging Technology for ISO 9001 Sustainability

Automation and **AI tools** are essential for maintaining and improving the QMS in a digital world. Technology can help streamline processes, track performance, and reduce the workload involved in managing the QMS.

- **Automation**: Implementing automation tools can help track performance indicators, conduct routine checks, and send reminders for audits and reviews. This reduces human error and ensures consistency.
- **Digital Platforms**: Using **cloud-based document management systems** allows for easier access to quality records, ensures document control, and promotes transparency across departments.

Technology	Description

Automation	Use automated systems for tracking and managing quality processes.
Digital Platforms	Implement cloud-based solutions for document management and communication.

Employee Involvement in Driving Change

For continuous improvement to be sustainable, all employees must feel engaged and empowered to make quality improvements. This requires fostering a culture where **employees at all levels** contribute to identifying inefficiencies and suggesting process improvements.

- **Training and Awareness**: Regular training and awareness sessions can help employees understand the importance of continuous improvement and their role in the process.
- **Ownership of Processes**: Empower employees to take ownership of specific processes. When employees own the outcomes of their work, they are more likely to suggest improvements and ensure quality standards are maintained.

Strategy	Description
Employee Training	Regular training programs to engage employees in the improvement process.
Ownership of Processes	Encourage employees to take responsibility for the quality of their work and suggest improvements.

4. Adapting the QMS to Future Changes in ISO 9001

ISO 9001 is a living standard that evolves over time. Organizations must be prepared for future revisions and updates to ensure the QMS remains aligned with **new ISO standards** and continues to deliver value.

Preparing for Future Revisions

The ISO 9001 standard is periodically reviewed and updated to reflect changes in global practices, customer expectations, and technological advances. Organizations must stay proactive and anticipate changes.

- **Stay Informed**: Regularly monitor updates to ISO 9001 to understand the implications for the organization's QMS.

- **Proactive Adaptation**: Incorporate potential changes into the strategic plans for QMS upgrades, ensuring smooth transitions when the standard is revised.

Aligning with New ISO Standards

Many organizations are adopting a **holistic approach** by integrating ISO 9001 with other management system standards, such as ISO 14001 (Environmental Management), ISO 45001 (Occupational Health and Safety), and ISO 27001 (Information Security Management).

- **Integrated Management System (IMS)**: Aligning multiple ISO standards into a single, cohesive system can streamline operations, reduce duplication, and improve overall management effectiveness.

Strategy	Description
Monitor ISO 9001 Changes	Stay updated on changes to ISO 9001 and adapt the QMS accordingly.
Integrated Management System	Align ISO 9001 with other relevant standards for a unified approach.

5. The Role of Leadership in Sustaining ISO 9001

Top management plays a crucial role in sustaining ISO 9001 certification. This section will emphasize the importance of leadership at every level of the organization in ensuring the long-term success of the QMS.

Top Management's Role Post-Certification

After certification, top management must continue to lead the QMS by ensuring its **effectiveness** and **alignment** with business objectives. Leadership must set the tone for continual improvement and compliance, fostering a culture that prioritizes quality at every level.

Leadership in Crisis Management

ISO 9001 also helps organizations manage crises by providing a structured approach for identifying risks and addressing issues. Leadership is crucial in ensuring that the QMS remains responsive during **emergencies** or unforeseen situations.

Leadership Role	Description

Post-Certification Leadership	Top management must continue to lead, review, and improve the QMS.
Crisis Management	Leaders must ensure the QMS supports crisis management and resilience.

6. Monitoring and Reviewing Performance to Ensure Compliance

Monitoring and reviewing the performance of the **Quality Management System (QMS)** is essential for maintaining ISO 9001 certification. It ensures that the QMS continues to meet its objectives, comply with **ISO 9001:2015 standards**, and drives continual improvement. Effective monitoring and review allow organizations to identify gaps, address nonconformities, and refine processes, ensuring that the QMS remains relevant and efficient over time.

The Importance of Ongoing Monitoring and Review

ISO 9001 requires organizations to monitor the **effectiveness** of their QMS and regularly review its performance. This is not just about ensuring compliance, but also about driving **continuous improvement**. Effective monitoring and review processes allow organizations to:

- Identify nonconformities and areas for improvement.
- Ensure the QMS continues to meet customer expectations and organizational goals.
- Stay aligned with **regulatory requirements** and **industry standards**.
- Measure the effectiveness of quality objectives and processes.
- Optimize resource allocation and operational efficiency.
- Adapt to changes in the business environment, customer needs, and market conditions.

Internal Audits as a Strategic Tool

Internal audits are a critical component of the ISO 9001 **monitoring and review** process. Traditionally, internal audits were seen as **compliance checks** to verify whether the organization was adhering to ISO 9001 standards. However, with the focus on **continuous improvement** in ISO 9001:2015, internal audits have evolved into **strategic tools** that provide valuable insights into the performance of the QMS.

Internal audits are no longer about just ensuring compliance; they are about identifying **risks**, **performance gaps**, and **areas for improvement**. By using internal audits strategically, organizations can enhance the effectiveness of the QMS and drive better business outcomes.

Strategic Role of Internal Audits:

1. **Identifying Risks and Gaps**:
   - Internal audits help identify potential risks in the QMS that could affect product quality or customer satisfaction. These risks can include bottlenecks, inefficiencies, and noncompliant practices that hinder performance.
   - Audits also help identify **gaps** in the current processes and **performance issues**, allowing the organization to take corrective actions before issues escalate.
2. **Fostering a Culture of Continuous Improvement**:
   - Internal audits promote a **proactive** approach to quality management. By identifying areas for improvement, audits can highlight opportunities to optimize processes, reduce waste, and enhance efficiency.
   - The results of internal audits can also help guide the **continuous improvement** cycle of the QMS, ensuring that the organization never becomes complacent but constantly strives to meet or exceed its objectives.
3. **Improving Compliance and Performance**:
   - Internal audits help ensure that the organization remains compliant with ISO 9001 standards, industry regulations, and customer expectations. Audits check whether processes are being followed correctly, and if not, corrective actions are implemented.
   - By identifying **performance gaps**, audits also help to address deficiencies that may affect customer satisfaction or operational effectiveness.
4. **Strategic Planning and Decision-Making**:
   - Internal audits can be incorporated into the organization's **strategic planning** process. The insights gained from audits inform decision-making and help management determine where resources should be allocated for improvement.
   - Audit findings can also guide **management reviews**, where top leadership assesses the effectiveness of the QMS and decides on future goals and initiatives.

How to Use Internal Audits to Enhance Performance

Organizations should use **internal audits** as a **strategic tool** to enhance the QMS and drive performance improvements. This requires a shift from simply checking for compliance to using audits as a mechanism for identifying areas that can contribute to business growth and customer satisfaction.

Steps for Strategic Internal Audits:

1. **Plan the Audit Process**:
    - Audit planning should align with the organization's **quality objectives** and strategic goals. This ensures that audits are focused on areas that have the greatest impact on the effectiveness of the QMS.
    - Audit teams should be trained not only to check compliance but also to identify opportunities for improvement.
2. **Review Key Processes**:
    - The audit should focus on key processes within the organization that affect product or service quality, such as **production**, **customer service**, **supply chain management**, and **resource management**.
    - Look beyond basic compliance; assess whether processes are effective, efficient, and aligned with business goals.
3. **Analyze Findings for Improvement**:
    - Audit findings should be analyzed to identify performance gaps and areas that require corrective actions. The goal is not just to find issues but to provide actionable insights that lead to improvements.
    - **Root cause analysis** should be conducted to determine the underlying causes of issues and address them effectively.
4. **Follow Up on Corrective Actions**:
    - After the audit, ensure that **corrective actions** are implemented and tracked. This could involve revising processes, updating documentation, or providing additional training.
    - Follow-up audits should verify whether corrective actions have been effective and whether the changes have led to performance improvements.
5. **Continuous Monitoring**:
    - Internal audits should be conducted regularly, with a continuous focus on monitoring process performance. This will help ensure that the QMS remains aligned with ISO 9001 requirements and that the organization is on track to meet its objectives.

Action	Description
Strategic Internal Audits	Use audits to evaluate QMS performance, not just compliance.
Focus on Key Processes	Audit critical processes to identify opportunities for improvement.
Root Cause Analysis	Investigate the causes of nonconformities and take corrective actions.
Continuous Monitoring	Regular audits ensure ongoing compliance and performance improvement.

Benefits of Using Internal Audits Strategically

By viewing internal audits as a tool for continuous improvement rather than just compliance, organizations can unlock numerous benefits:

Benefit	Description
Improved Performance	Audits help identify and address performance gaps, leading to better operational outcomes.
Enhanced Compliance	Regular audits ensure that the QMS remains compliant with ISO 9001 and regulatory requirements.
Increased Efficiency	Identifying inefficiencies during audits helps streamline processes and reduce waste.
Better Decision-Making	Audit findings provide valuable data for management reviews and strategic decision-making.
Stronger Customer Satisfaction	Audits help identify and resolve issues that may affect product or service quality, improving customer satisfaction.

Conclusion

Internal audits are a vital tool for ensuring ISO 9001 compliance, but they can also serve as a strategic tool for improving the QMS. By focusing on performance gaps, risk identification, and continuous improvement, audits help organizations move beyond mere compliance checks. Strategic internal audits contribute to the **long-term success** of the QMS by driving efficiency, improving decision-making, and ensuring that the organization consistently meets customer expectations and ISO 9001 standards.

CHAPTER 3

Starting Your Quality Management Journey

INTRODUCTION

Starting the journey toward **ISO 9001 certification** and implementing a **Quality Management System (QMS)** is a significant commitment for any organization, especially for small enterprises. Before diving into the complexities of the standard and the implementation process, it is essential to assess the **organizational readiness**. Understanding where the organization stands in terms of quality management, culture, and resources is crucial for successful implementation and long-term sustainability of the QMS.

Assessing organizational readiness involves evaluating current processes, understanding gaps in the existing system, and determining the resources, leadership, and commitment needed to integrate ISO 9001 effectively. This chapter will guide you through the steps to assess your organization's readiness to implement and sustain ISO 9001, ensuring a smooth transition and successful certification.

1. Assessing Current Quality Management Practices

The first step in assessing readiness is evaluating the **current state** of your organization's quality management practices. This assessment helps identify what is already in place, where improvements are needed, and the potential challenges your business may face in implementing ISO 9001.

Key Areas to Evaluate:

- **Existing Quality Management Practices**:

Review any existing quality management practices, policies, and procedures. Determine if these align with the principles of ISO 9001 and if they can be adapted to fit the standard.

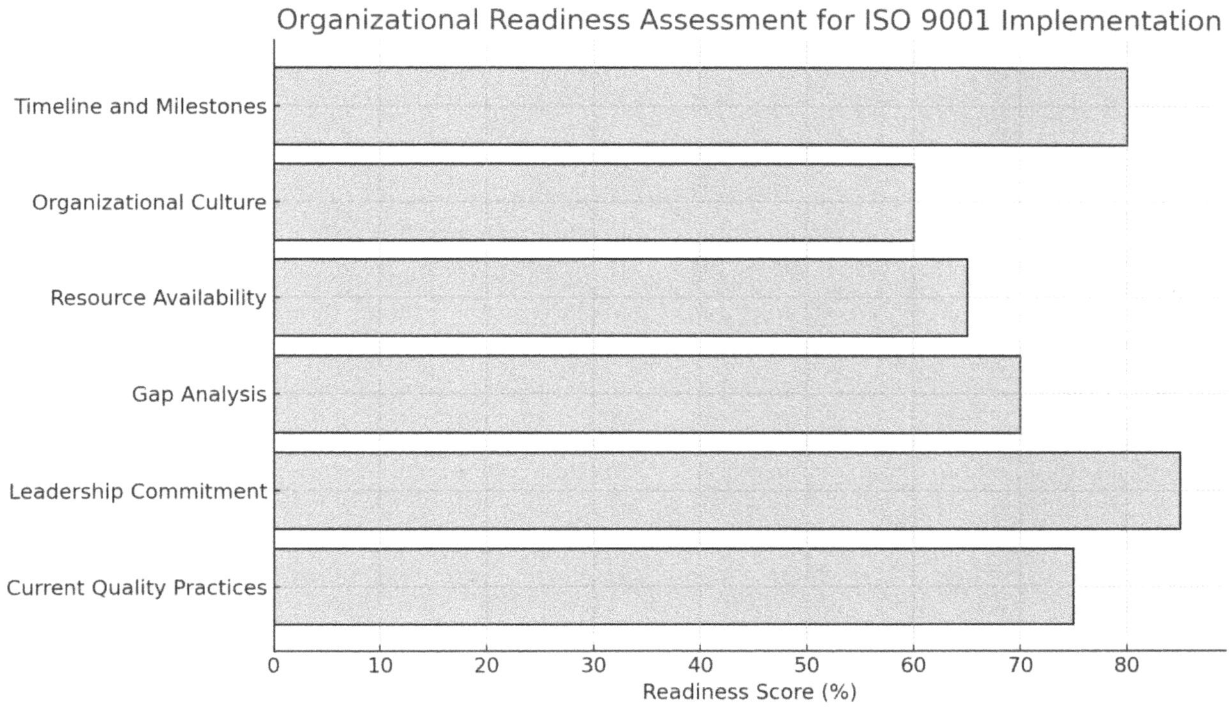

- **Compliance with Customer Requirements**:

  Assess how well the organization currently meets customer expectations and whether there are gaps in meeting customer satisfaction or requirements.

- **Documented Information**:

  Evaluate existing documentation (procedures, records, and manuals). ISO 9001 requires specific documented information; determine if your current documentation is sufficient or needs revision.

- **Employee Involvement**:

  Assess how employees currently engage with quality-related processes. Are they trained? Are they actively participating in quality initiatives?

Benefits:

- Identifies strengths and weaknesses in the current quality management system.
- Provides insight into the readiness for formalizing processes.
- Helps avoid redundant efforts by focusing on areas that need improvement.

2. Engaging Leadership and Securing Commitment

ISO 9001:2015 places significant emphasis on **leadership involvement**. Top management must be fully engaged and committed to the quality management journey. Leadership plays a pivotal role in setting the vision for the QMS, providing necessary resources, and ensuring that the QMS is aligned with organizational objectives.

Key Actions for Leadership:

- **Commitment to Quality**:

  Leaders must demonstrate a genuine commitment to quality. This includes setting clear objectives, aligning quality initiatives with business goals, and encouraging employee involvement in the process.

- **Providing Resources and Support**:

  The leadership must allocate the necessary resources, including human resources, financial support, and infrastructure, to ensure the successful implementation and maintenance of the QMS.

- **Setting the Right Culture**:

  Top management must cultivate a **quality-driven culture** where continuous improvement and customer satisfaction are prioritized.

Benefits:

- Strong leadership ensures that the QMS is not just a compliance exercise but a core part of the organization's operations.
- Ensures that the QMS is aligned with business strategy and objectives.

- Helps secure buy-in from all levels of the organization, making the QMS more effective.

3. Conducting a Gap Analysis

A **gap analysis** is a systematic assessment of the differences between the organization's current quality practices and the requirements outlined in ISO 9001. This step helps identify the areas that need improvement or additional effort to achieve ISO 9001 compliance.

Key Steps in Conducting a Gap Analysis:

1. **Understand ISO 9001 Requirements**:

   Study the ISO 9001 standard and its requirements. Familiarize yourself with the clauses and key principles.

2. **Evaluate Current Processes**:

   Review existing processes, procedures, and documentation to assess their alignment with ISO 9001 requirements. Identify areas where the organization is already compliant and where gaps exist.

3. **Document Findings**:

   Document the areas of non-compliance and areas for improvement. Create a roadmap of actions to address the gaps.

Benefits:

- Helps create a clear plan for achieving ISO 9001 compliance.
- Identifies areas that need immediate attention and improvement.
- Provides clarity on the scope of the work required for certification.

4. Assessing Resource Availability

Implementing a QMS requires adequate resources, both in terms of **human resources** and **financial investment**. It's important to assess whether the organization has the necessary resources to implement and sustain ISO 9001.

Key Resources to Assess:

- **Human Resources**:

  Evaluate the skills and competencies of employees, especially those involved in quality management processes. Determine if additional training or hiring is required.

- **Training and Development**:

  Assess current employee training programs and their alignment with ISO 9001 requirements. Ensure that staff at all levels are knowledgeable about the QMS and their roles within it.

- **Financial Resources**:

  Review the budget required for the implementation of the QMS, including costs for documentation, training, audits, and certification fees.

- **Infrastructure**:
  Ensure that the physical infrastructure (equipment, facilities, technology) supports the QMS processes and is compliant with the requirements of ISO 9001.

Benefits:

- Helps in identifying any **resource gaps** early on.
- Ensures that adequate investments are made in training, technology, and processes.
- Helps ensure the sustainability of the QMS over time.

5. Understanding Organizational Culture and Readiness for Change

ISO 9001 requires a cultural shift towards **quality** and **continuous improvement**. Before implementing the standard, it's important to evaluate the organization's readiness for change.

Key Cultural Aspects to Consider:

- **Employee Buy-In**:

  Evaluate the readiness of employees to embrace change. Are they committed to improving quality? Are they willing to participate in QMS processes?

- **Change Management**:

  Assess how the organization manages change. Are employees open to adopting new processes and procedures? Is there resistance to change?

- **Communication**:

  Ensure that there are clear communication channels within the organization to discuss the benefits of ISO 9001 and address concerns.

Benefits:

- Helps prepare the workforce for the changes that ISO 9001 will bring.
- Identifies potential sources of resistance and addresses them proactively.
- Ensures that the QMS becomes part of the organization's culture, rather than just a compliance task.

6. Determining the Timeline and Milestones

Implementing ISO 9001 is a project that requires careful planning. Once the organization's readiness is assessed, it's important to develop a **timeline** with clear milestones to guide the implementation process.

Key Steps for Timeline and Milestones:

1. **Set Clear Goals and Objectives**:

   Define what success looks like at each stage of the implementation process, including certification.

2. **Establish a Timeline**:

Develop a realistic timeline for achieving key milestones, such as **documenting processes**, **training employees**, and **conducting internal audits**.

3. **Monitor Progress**:

   Regularly monitor progress toward the implementation milestones and adjust the timeline as necessary.

Benefits:

- Provides clear direction and deadlines, reducing uncertainty.
- Helps allocate resources effectively and ensures accountability.
- Keeps the organization on track to achieve ISO 9001 certification within a reasonable timeframe.

Conclusion

Assessing your organization's readiness for ISO 9001 implementation is an essential first step in the certification process. By evaluating the current quality management practices, securing leadership commitment, conducting a gap analysis, ensuring resource availability, and preparing for change, your organization can set the foundation for a successful QMS implementation.

The readiness assessment provides the clarity and structure needed to navigate the complexity of ISO 9001, ensuring that small businesses can achieve certification and maintain a high standard of quality management that supports long-term growth and success.

Initial Steps for ISO 9001 Implementation

Implementing **ISO 9001:2015** in any organization, particularly small enterprises, can seem like a complex task. However, with a well-planned approach, the process can be broken down into manageable steps. The key to a successful implementation lies in the initial steps taken before the actual work begins. These steps ensure that the organization is prepared and positioned for effective adoption of the **Quality Management System (QMS)**.

Below, we explain the **initial steps** involved in implementing ISO 9001, focusing on the core activities that lay the foundation for a successful certification process.

1. Understand ISO 9001 Requirements

Before starting the implementation process, the first step is to **understand the ISO 9001:2015 requirements**. This includes familiarizing yourself with the **clauses** and the **principles** behind the standard. It's important to recognize that ISO 9001 is a framework, not a one-size-fits-all solution. Therefore, it should be adapted to fit the unique needs and structure of the organization.

Step	Description
Understand the Standard	Review and familiarize yourself with the ISO 9001:2015 clauses and their application.
Define Key Principles	Embrace the **quality principles** that drive ISO 9001:2015, such as customer focus, leadership, and continuous improvement.

2. Secure Leadership Commitment

ISO 9001 implementation requires strong **commitment from top management**. Leadership involvement is critical because the success of the **Quality Management System (QMS)** relies on the resources, strategic direction, and organizational culture set by leadership. Management must actively support and commit to the implementation process by providing the necessary resources, setting quality objectives, and ensuring organizational alignment.

Step	Description
Engage Top Management	Ensure that leadership understands the importance of ISO 9001 and is committed to supporting the implementation process.
Allocate Resources	Management should ensure that necessary resources (financial, human, and time) are provided for implementation.

3. Establish a Project Team

Once leadership is on board, it is crucial to form a **project team**. This team is responsible for driving the implementation process. The team should include individuals with knowledge of the organization's processes, an understanding of quality management, and the ability to engage other employees.

Step	Description

Form a Project Team	Create a team with cross-functional members to lead the ISO 9001 implementation.
Designate Roles	Assign clear roles and responsibilities within the project team to ensure accountability.

4. Conduct a Gap Analysis

A **gap analysis** is a critical step in understanding the difference between the organization's existing practices and the requirements of ISO 9001:2015. This analysis helps identify areas that need improvement and sets the foundation for creating an action plan to close these gaps.

Step	Description
Evaluate Existing Systems	Review existing processes and procedures to identify gaps between current practices and ISO 9001 requirements.
Create a Gap Action Plan	Develop an action plan to address the gaps, specifying the changes and improvements required.

5. Develop a Quality Policy and Objectives

ISO 9001 requires organizations to develop a **Quality Policy** that aligns with the strategic direction of the business. The policy should communicate the organization's commitment to quality and outline its quality goals. Alongside the policy, clear **quality objectives** should be set to ensure measurable progress toward meeting customer needs and achieving continual improvement.

Step	Description
Develop Quality Policy	Create a quality policy that reflects the organization's commitment to quality.
Set Quality Objectives	Establish measurable quality objectives that align with the business strategy and customer requirements.

6. Plan the QMS Structure

Planning the structure of the **Quality Management System (QMS)** is essential for its effective implementation. This includes determining what processes need to be documented, how documentation will be controlled, and how responsibilities will be allocated. The QMS should be designed to fit the needs of the organization and support the achievement of the quality objectives.

Step	Description
Identify Key Processes	Define the key processes that impact quality, such as product design, production, and customer service.
Develop QMS Documentation	Plan the documentation required to support the QMS, including procedures, work instructions, and records.

7. Provide Training and Raise Awareness

Training is essential to ensure that employees understand the principles of ISO 9001 and their role in the QMS. Additionally, raising awareness across the organization helps to foster a **quality-driven culture**. Everyone in the organization should understand the impact of their work on quality, customer satisfaction, and organizational success.

Step	Description
Conduct Employee Training	Provide training for employees on the basics of ISO 9001, the QMS, and their roles in achieving quality objectives.
Raise Awareness	Ensure that all employees understand the importance of quality management and how it contributes to business success.

8. Monitor and Review Progress

Once the implementation begins, it's important to regularly **monitor progress** to ensure that the implementation is on track. This involves conducting periodic reviews of the action plan, measuring performance against quality objectives, and identifying areas where additional efforts are needed.

Step	Description
Monitor Implementation	Regularly check progress against set objectives and timelines.
Conduct Reviews	Review progress with the project team and leadership to ensure that the implementation is moving forward.

Conclusion

Implementing ISO 9001 is a structured process that requires careful planning, commitment, and active participation from all levels of the organization. By following these **initial steps**, small enterprises can lay a strong foundation for a **successful QMS implementation**. Understanding the ISO 9001 requirements, engaging leadership, conducting a gap analysis, and setting clear objectives are essential first steps that set the stage for a robust and sustainable **Quality Management System**.

These foundational steps not only guide the certification process but also ensure that the QMS becomes an integral part of the organization's culture, continuously driving improvement and meeting customer expectations.

Engaging Top Management

Engaging top management is essential for the successful implementation and maintenance of **ISO 9001:2015**. The leadership team must demonstrate active commitment and involvement in every stage of the **Quality Management System (QMS)** development, ensuring that quality management is not just a compliance task but a strategic initiative that supports the overall business goals.

Top management plays a central role in driving the quality culture, providing resources, and aligning the QMS with the organization's objectives. Their active participation ensures that the system is not only implemented but sustained and improved over time.

Here are some key responsibilities and actions for top management in engaging with ISO 9001 implementation:

Key Responsibilities of Top Management in ISO 9001 Implementation

Responsibility	Description
Commitment to Quality	Top management must visibly demonstrate their commitment to quality. This involves setting the tone for the quality culture within the organization.
Establishing the Quality Policy	Management must define a **quality policy** that reflects the organization's commitment to meeting customer requirements and ensuring continual improvement.
Setting Quality Objectives	Top management is responsible for setting **clear, measurable quality objectives** that align with the organization's strategic goals and customer expectations.
Allocating Resources	Ensuring that adequate resources (financial, human, and technological) are provided to establish, implement, and maintain the QMS.
Monitoring and Reviewing QMS Performance	Management must regularly review the performance of the QMS, ensuring it aligns with business goals and is continually improving.

Fostering a Quality-Centric Culture	Creating a culture that values quality at all levels of the organization, ensuring that quality is a part of the organizational DNA.
Providing Leadership	Top management must provide clear leadership, inspiring the entire organization to adopt the QMS and actively contribute to quality management initiatives.

Top Management's Role in Establishing the QMS Framework

1. **Leadership and Commitment**

   Top management must lead by example. Their involvement in the QMS shows that quality management is a top priority, which encourages all levels of the organization to follow suit. Management's leadership ensures that quality initiatives are adequately prioritized and resourced.

2. **Establishing a Clear Vision for Quality**

   Top management is responsible for **defining the organization's vision** regarding quality and ensuring that it aligns with the overall **strategic objectives** of the business. This vision should be reflected in the **quality policy** and integrated into the business strategy.

3. **Ensuring the Allocation of Necessary Resources**

   A successful QMS requires adequate resources. Top management must ensure that the necessary financial, human, and technological resources are available to implement and maintain the QMS effectively. This includes providing training, tools, and infrastructure to support quality management.

4. **Setting and Communicating Quality Objectives**

   Quality objectives should be **specific, measurable, achievable, relevant, and time-bound** (SMART). Top management is responsible for setting these objectives at the organizational level, ensuring they align with customer requirements and overall business goals.

Engagement in Ongoing QMS Performance and Improvement

1. **Monitoring and Reviewing QMS Effectiveness**

   ISO 9001 requires ongoing evaluation of the QMS to ensure its continued effectiveness. Top management must regularly review the performance of the QMS through **management reviews**, assessing the achievement of quality objectives, addressing nonconformities, and identifying areas for improvement.

2. **Providing Continuous Improvement Leadership**

   Continual improvement is one of the core principles of ISO 9001. Top management must not only support improvement initiatives but also lead them. This involves actively seeking opportunities for improvement and ensuring that corrective actions are taken when issues arise.

3. **Supporting Internal and External Audits**

   Internal audits are a key part of ISO 9001, ensuring that processes are in compliance with the standard. Top management should actively support internal audits, participate in **audit reviews**, and ensure that **nonconformities** are addressed effectively.

4. **Encouraging Cross-Departmental Collaboration**

   Quality management should be a **cross-functional effort**. Top management needs to foster collaboration between departments to ensure that quality initiatives are integrated into all aspects of the organization, from product design to customer service.

Benefits of Engaging Top Management in ISO 9001 Implementation

Engaging top management has several benefits for the successful implementation of the QMS:

Benefit	**Description**
Clear Direction and Commitment	Top management provides a clear direction for the QMS, ensuring that the organization's objectives are

	aligned with customer expectations and strategic goals.
Access to Resources	Management ensures that sufficient resources (funding, personnel, technology) are allocated to maintain and improve the QMS.
Improved Alignment with Business Strategy	The involvement of top management ensures that the QMS is aligned with the organization's overall business strategy, increasing its relevance and impact.
Sustained Commitment to Continual Improvement	Leadership ensures a focus on continual improvement by setting goals, reviewing progress, and driving change based on data and performance metrics.
Enhanced Employee Engagement and Buy-In	When top management is visibly involved, employees are more likely to engage with the QMS and understand the importance of quality management in achieving success.

Conclusion

Engaging top management is the foundation for the success of ISO 9001:2015 implementation. Leadership involvement ensures that the QMS is aligned with the organization's strategic objectives, is well-resourced, and is continuously improved. Without strong leadership, the QMS may lack the support and direction needed to be effective.

Top management's commitment to quality and their leadership throughout the implementation process ensures that quality management becomes an integral part of the organization's culture, leading to improved customer satisfaction, better operational efficiency, and long-term success.

CHAPTER 4

Setting the Foundation for the QMS

DEFINING ORGANIZATIONAL CONTEXT

In **ISO 9001:2015**, defining the **organizational context** is a foundational step for building an effective **Quality Management System (QMS)**. Understanding and evaluating the internal and external factors that can impact the QMS is crucial for ensuring that the system is aligned with the organization's objectives and capable of addressing both challenges and opportunities.

Defining organizational context allows businesses, particularly small enterprises, to establish a **tailored approach** to quality management. It ensures that the QMS is not generic but instead reflects the unique challenges and goals of the organization. By thoroughly assessing the context, organizations can ensure that their QMS is relevant, responsive, and aligned with strategic priorities.

What is Organizational Context in ISO 9001?

Organizational context refers to the understanding of **internal and external factors** that influence how an organization operates and how the QMS should be structured and implemented. This involves considering:

- The **environment** in which the organization operates.
- The **stakeholders** and their expectations.
- The **resources** available to the organization.
- The **risks and opportunities** that may affect the ability to achieve quality objectives and improve the system.

By understanding these elements, an organization can make informed decisions about how to design and manage its QMS to ensure it is effective and continually improving.

Steps to Define Organizational Context

The process of defining organizational context involves several steps that help businesses identify and understand the factors affecting their QMS. These steps guide organizations in creating a system that is both aligned with their strategic goals and adaptable to changing circumstances.

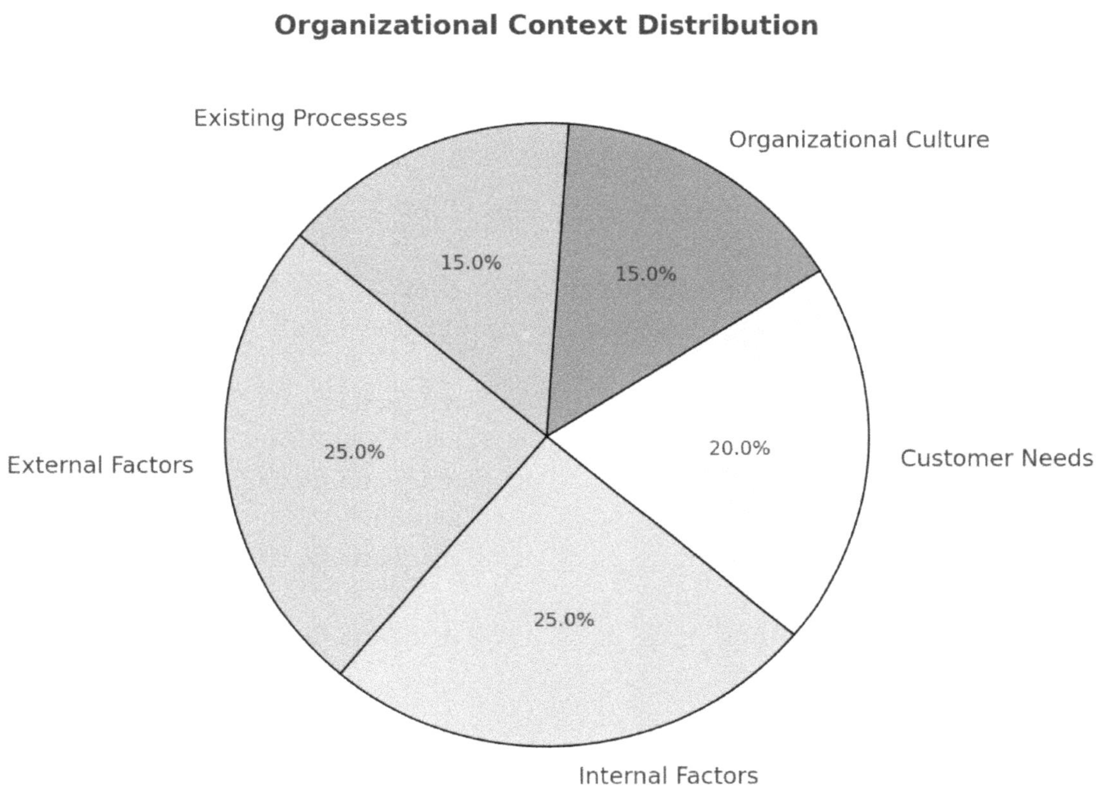

1. Understand the External and Internal Factors

Organizations must evaluate both **internal** and **external factors** that can affect the QMS. External factors include market conditions, customer needs, regulatory requirements, and technological advancements, while internal factors include the organization's culture, structure, capabilities, and processes.

External Factors:

- **Economic Conditions**: Changes in the economy can impact the availability of resources and customer expectations.

- **Regulations and Compliance**: Legal and regulatory requirements can influence how products or services are delivered.
- **Market Trends and Customer Needs**: Shifting customer expectations and competitive pressures may affect the demand for certain products or services.

Internal Factors:

- **Organizational Structure**: The structure of the company, including its departments and decision-making processes, will affect how the QMS is designed.
- **Organizational Culture**: The values and behaviors within the organization, including attitudes toward quality and innovation, shape how the QMS is implemented.
- **Current Processes**: The organization's existing processes must be assessed to identify opportunities for integration with the QMS.

External Factors	Internal Factors
Economic conditions and market forces	Organizational structure and leadership
Legal and regulatory requirements	Corporate culture and employee engagement
Customer needs and satisfaction expectations	Existing processes and resource availability
Technological advancements and innovations	Infrastructure, facilities, and equipment

2. Identify and Analyze Interested Parties

An essential part of defining organizational context is understanding the needs and expectations of **interested parties**—also known as stakeholders. These are individuals or groups that can affect, be affected by, or perceive themselves to be affected by the organization's activities and the QMS.

Interested Parties May Include:

- **Customers**: Their needs and expectations are central to the QMS.
- **Suppliers**: Relationships with suppliers influence product quality and availability.
- **Employees**: The skills, involvement, and commitment of employees are essential for quality management.

- **Regulatory Bodies**: Compliance with laws, standards, and regulations is required.
- **Shareholders or Investors**: Their interests are often tied to the organization's performance and success.

By identifying the stakeholders and understanding their needs, organizations can align their QMS to meet both customer and business requirements effectively.

Interested Parties	Expectations
Customers	Quality products/services, timely delivery, customer support
Suppliers	Clear communication, timely payments, fair partnership
Employees	Training, engagement, and opportunities for growth
Regulatory Bodies	Compliance with relevant laws and standards
Shareholders	Business sustainability, profitability, and growth

3. Define the Scope of the QMS

Once the internal and external factors and interested parties are understood, the next step is to define the **scope** of the QMS. The scope refers to the areas of the organization that will be covered by the QMS, ensuring that the system addresses all relevant processes, risks, and opportunities.

Defining the scope involves:

- **Determining Boundaries**: Which departments, processes, or products will be included in the QMS.
- **Assessing Relevance**: Understanding which aspects of the business are critical to quality management and aligning the scope accordingly.
- **Documenting the Scope**: The scope must be documented and communicated to ensure clarity across the organization.

The scope should be flexible, allowing the QMS to grow and evolve as the organization's needs change.

Scope Definition	Considerations
Defining boundaries of QMS coverage	Which departments, locations, and processes will be included?
Ensuring the scope is aligned with strategic goals	Are the right quality objectives and customer needs addressed?

Documenting and communicating the scope	Clarity across the organization about the QMS's scope

4. Identify Risks and Opportunities

A key component of ISO 9001:2015 is the adoption of **risk-based thinking**. The organization must assess potential risks and opportunities that may affect its ability to achieve the desired outcomes of the QMS.

Key Steps in Risk Assessment:

- **Identify Risks**: Recognize possible risks that could affect product or service quality, such as supply chain disruptions or regulatory changes.
- **Assess the Impact**: Evaluate the likelihood and potential impact of these risks.
- **Implement Preventive Actions**: Develop actions to mitigate risks and capitalize on opportunities to enhance the QMS.

Risk management helps ensure that the organization is prepared for potential disruptions and can maintain consistent performance despite challenges.

Risk Management	Description
Identify potential risks	Recognize potential internal and external risks.
Assess risks based on likelihood and impact	Evaluate the probability and severity of risks.
Implement actions to mitigate risks	Develop preventive actions to address identified risks.

5. Communicate and Align the QMS with Strategic Goals

Once the context is understood, it's important to ensure that the QMS is aligned with the organization's **strategic objectives**. The QMS should support the overall business strategy and help the organization achieve its goals.

Communication is vital in this phase to ensure that all employees understand the QMS's purpose and how it contributes to the business's success. Leadership must clearly communicate the connection between quality management and business objectives, promoting buy-in and engagement from all employees.

Key Considerations	Actions
Aligning QMS with business strategy	Ensure that the QMS objectives reflect organizational goals.
Clear communication across the organization	Ensure all employees understand the purpose of the QMS and their role in it.
Management commitment to the QMS and strategic goals	Top management must actively support and lead the QMS initiative.

Conclusion

Defining the organizational context is an essential first step in **implementing ISO 9001**. By understanding the **external and internal factors**, identifying **interested parties**, defining the **scope of the QMS**, assessing **risks and opportunities**, and aligning the QMS with the **strategic goals**, small enterprises can ensure their QMS is relevant, effective, and adaptable. This foundational step sets the stage for a successful QMS that drives improvement, meets customer expectations, and supports the organization's long-term success.

Understanding Stakeholder Needs and Expectations

Understanding stakeholder needs and expectations is a crucial component of implementing ISO 9001:2015. A stakeholder is any individual or group that has an interest in the performance and activities of the organization. Stakeholders can include customers, employees, suppliers, regulatory bodies, investors, and even the community at large.

Understanding these needs and expectations helps ensure that the **Quality Management System (QMS)** is aligned with the expectations of those who affect or are affected by the organization's products, services, and operations. ISO 9001 emphasizes the importance of considering these factors when developing and implementing the QMS to ensure that the organization consistently meets or exceeds these expectations.

Steps to Understand Stakeholder Needs and Expectations:

1. **Identify Stakeholders**:

   The first step is to identify all stakeholders. This includes both **internal** (employees, management) and **external** (customers, suppliers, regulatory bodies) parties. The QMS must consider their influence on the organization and how their needs align with the company's objectives.

2. **Determine Stakeholder Expectations**:

   Once stakeholders are identified, the next step is to determine what each stakeholder expects from the organization. For customers, this might include product quality, timely delivery, and customer service. For suppliers, it might involve clear communication, on-time payments, and long-term partnerships.

3. **Monitor Changes in Expectations**:

   Stakeholder expectations can evolve over time. It's crucial to continually monitor these changes and adapt the QMS to ensure it remains aligned with the shifting needs of stakeholders.

4. **Integrate Stakeholder Needs into the QMS**:

   The needs and expectations of stakeholders should influence the creation of quality objectives, risk management strategies, and product/service delivery processes. By integrating these needs into the QMS, the organization can ensure it delivers products and services that satisfy stakeholder requirements.

Stakeholder	Needs/Expectations
Customers	Product quality, customer service, on-time delivery, value
Employees	Job security, development opportunities, good working conditions
Suppliers	Timely payments, long-term contracts, clear communication
Regulatory Bodies	Compliance with laws and regulations, transparency
Investors	Return on investment, business growth, stability

Benefits:

- Helps the organization align its operations with market demands and expectations.
- Ensures higher levels of customer satisfaction and loyalty.
- Facilitates compliance with regulations and industry standards.
- Builds trust and stronger relationships with stakeholders.

Setting Clear Quality Objectives

Setting **clear quality objectives** is a key requirement in ISO 9001:2015. These objectives are specific, measurable targets that the organization aims to achieve to improve the quality of its processes, products, and services. Quality objectives help the organization monitor its progress, assess performance, and ensure alignment with the overall business strategy and customer satisfaction.

Key Aspects of Setting Clear Quality Objectives:

1. **Alignment with Strategic Goals**:

   Quality objectives must be aligned with the organization's overall strategic direction and business goals. This ensures that quality management directly supports the company's growth, profitability, and customer satisfaction.

2. **SMART Criteria**:

   Quality objectives should be **SMART—Specific**, **Measurable**, **Achievable**, **Relevant**, and **Time-bound**. This ensures that the objectives are clear and can be effectively tracked over time.

   - **Specific**: Clearly define what is to be achieved.
   - **Measurable**: Ensure there is a way to track progress or performance.
   - **Achievable**: Set realistic goals that are within reach.
   - **Relevant**: Ensure the objectives align with the company's mission and stakeholder needs.
   - **Time-bound**: Set a clear timeline for achieving the objectives.
3. **Types of Quality Objectives**:
   - **Customer-Focused**: Objectives that improve customer satisfaction, such as reducing customer complaints or improving product delivery times.
   - **Operational Efficiency**: Objectives that focus on improving internal processes, such as reducing defects or increasing process efficiency.
   - **Compliance and Risk Management**: Objectives that ensure the organization meets legal, regulatory, and safety requirements.

- **Continuous Improvement**: Objectives aimed at continually improving the QMS, such as increasing employee training or reducing product recall rates.

4. **Monitoring and Review**:

   Once quality objectives are set, it's important to monitor performance against these objectives. Regular reviews help identify gaps or areas for improvement and ensure that the objectives remain relevant as the organization grows and evolves.

Quality Objective	Description	Target/Metric
Customer Satisfaction	Improve customer satisfaction by reducing complaints	Reduce customer complaints by 20%
Operational Efficiency	Increase efficiency in production by reducing waste	Reduce waste in production by 15%
Compliance	Ensure 100% compliance with environmental regulations	Achieve zero environmental nonconformities
Employee Engagement	Increase employee involvement in quality initiatives	90% employee participation in quality programs

Conclusion

Understanding **stakeholder needs and expectations** and **setting clear quality objectives** are two crucial aspects of building an effective **Quality Management System (QMS)**. By identifying what stakeholders require and aligning the organization's quality objectives with those needs, businesses can ensure their QMS remains focused on customer satisfaction and continuous improvement.

Setting clear and measurable quality objectives ensures that the organization can track progress, evaluate performance, and continuously align its operations with business goals. These practices not only support ISO 9001 compliance but also drive long-term business success through improved operational efficiency, customer satisfaction, and stakeholder engagement.

CHAPTER 5

Planning the QMS Implementation

CREATING AN IMPLEMENTATION PLAN

Creating a **Quality Management System (QMS) implementation plan** is one of the most crucial steps in the journey toward achieving ISO 9001 certification. This plan provides a structured approach for rolling out the QMS across the organization, ensuring that all requirements of ISO 9001 are addressed systematically. A well-crafted implementation plan acts as a roadmap, guiding the organization through each stage of the process—from initial planning to final certification and beyond.

An effective QMS implementation plan helps ensure that the organization is aligned with the **ISO 9001:2015** standard, minimizes the risk of non-compliance, and facilitates continuous improvement. Below is a detailed explanation of how to create an **implementation plan** for ISO 9001.

Key Steps to Creating a QMS Implementation Plan

1. Define Objectives and Scope

The first step in creating an implementation plan is to **define the objectives** of the QMS and the **scope** of the implementation. This ensures that the plan aligns with both **business goals** and **ISO 9001 requirements**.

- **Objectives**: The implementation plan should begin by identifying the specific quality objectives that the QMS aims to achieve. These could include improving customer satisfaction, reducing operational costs, ensuring compliance, or enhancing product quality.
- **Scope**: The scope defines which parts of the organization will be included in the QMS. This could involve one department, the entire organization, or

specific products/services. Defining the scope ensures that the QMS addresses all relevant aspects of the organization's operations.

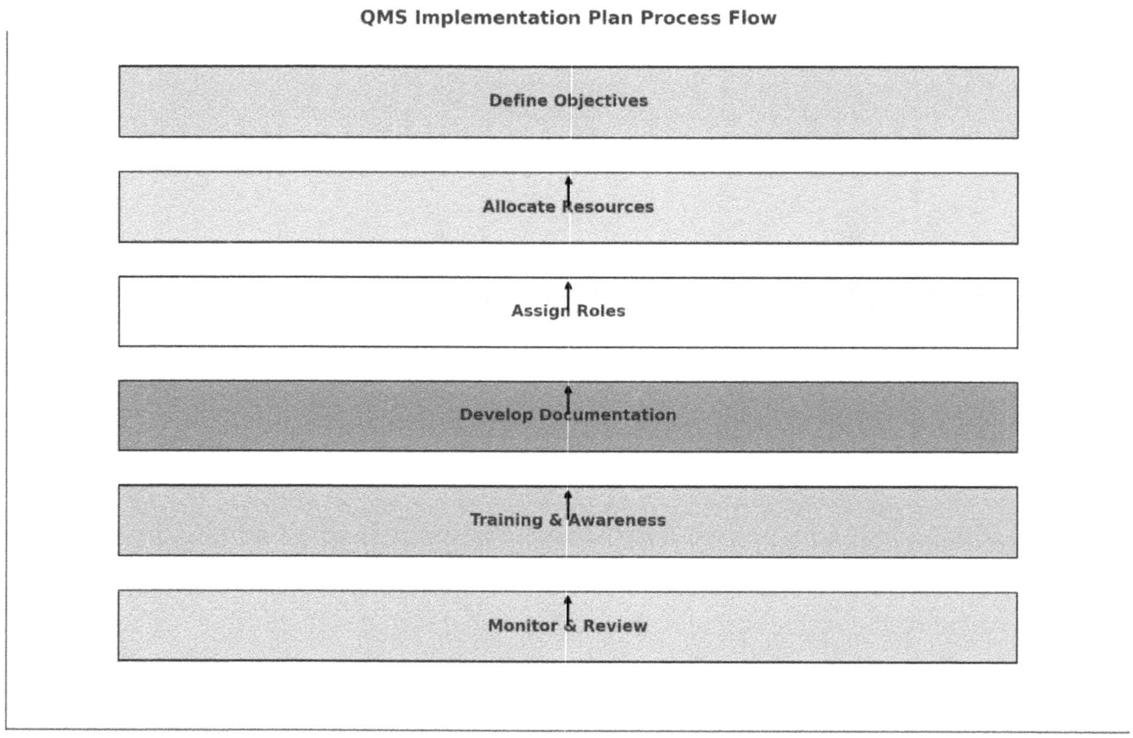

Action	Description
Define QMS Objectives	Set clear and measurable quality objectives that align with business goals.
Determine Scope	Specify the boundaries and areas of the organization to be covered by the QMS.

2. Assign Responsibilities

An essential part of the implementation plan is to assign roles and responsibilities to ensure that every aspect of the QMS is effectively managed. This includes designating a **project team** responsible for implementing the QMS, as well as determining who will oversee specific tasks.

- **Project Team**: Select individuals with the right expertise to manage the implementation process. The team should include people from different functions and departments within the organization (e.g., operations, quality, HR, IT).

- **Assigning Roles**: For each element of the QMS, designate responsible individuals to ensure that activities are carried out on time and to the required standard. This could include individuals responsible for documentation, internal audits, employee training, and customer feedback management.

Action	Description
Form a Project Team	Create a team with representatives from all relevant departments.
Assign Specific Roles	Designate clear responsibilities for each task involved in the implementation.

3. Develop a Timeline and Milestones

Creating a realistic **timeline** is essential to keep the implementation on track and ensure that all ISO 9001 requirements are met. The timeline should outline the specific **milestones** or key activities that must be achieved to successfully implement the QMS.

- **Phases**: Break the implementation process into manageable phases. Each phase should focus on a specific aspect of the QMS, such as planning, training, documentation, or internal audits.
- **Milestones**: Set clear milestones within each phase to track progress. These milestones could include document creation, employee training sessions, completion of internal audits, and final management reviews.

Action	Description
Set a Realistic Timeline	Define a clear, achievable timeline for each stage of QMS implementation.
Identify Key Milestones	Break the timeline into milestones to track progress and ensure timely completion.

4. Allocate Resources

Effective implementation requires adequate **resources**, including financial, human, and technological support. In this step, the organization needs to identify and allocate the resources needed to implement the QMS successfully.

- **Human Resources**: Ensure that the right people are available for the implementation process. This may involve **training** employees, hiring additional staff, or engaging external consultants.
- **Financial Resources**: Establish the budget for the entire implementation process, covering costs for documentation, training, software, certification fees, and internal audits.
- **Technological Resources**: Determine if any new systems or tools are needed, such as document management software or internal audit systems.

Action	Description
Allocate Financial Resources	Ensure that the required budget is available for implementation.
Ensure Human Resources	Assign employees, provide training, or hire consultants as necessary.
Provide Technological Support	Identify and allocate necessary tools and technology for QMS implementation.

5. Identify Key Processes and Documentation Needs

ISO 9001 requires that processes are defined, documented, and controlled. As part of the implementation plan, organizations must identify the key processes within their operations that need to be documented.

- **Process Mapping**: Identify the critical processes that affect product quality and customer satisfaction, such as procurement, production, and customer support. These processes must be documented and continuously monitored.
- **Documentation Requirements**: ISO 9001 requires certain documents, including a **quality manual**, **procedures**, and **work instructions**. Develop these documents to ensure they are comprehensive and compliant with ISO standards.

Action	Description
Identify Key Processes	Map and define the key processes affecting quality management.
Create and Control Documents	Develop the required documentation and implement a document control system.

6. Training and Awareness

Training is a critical aspect of QMS implementation. Employees at all levels must be familiar with the **ISO 9001 requirements**, their roles in the QMS, and how to use the quality management system effectively.

- **Employee Training**: Provide training for employees on the QMS, quality objectives, and their specific responsibilities. This can include workshops, online courses, and hands-on sessions.
- **Raising Awareness**: Beyond training, it is crucial to raise awareness about the importance of quality management throughout the organization. Employees must understand that quality is everyone's responsibility.

Action	Description
Provide Training	Train employees on ISO 9001, the QMS, and their roles in quality management.
Raise Awareness	Foster a quality-oriented culture by engaging employees in QMS activities.

7. Monitor Progress and Review

To ensure that the QMS implementation is on track, regular monitoring and reviews are essential. Set up a system for **performance evaluation** and **progress tracking**.

- **Internal Audits**: Conduct internal audits regularly to assess compliance with the QMS, identify areas for improvement, and make corrective actions as necessary.
- **Management Review**: Top management should regularly review the status of QMS implementation, ensuring it aligns with business goals and customer requirements.

Action	Description
Monitor Implementation	Track progress against objectives and timelines to ensure success.
Conduct Regular Audits	Perform internal audits to evaluate the effectiveness of the QMS.
Management Review	Ensure top management reviews and assesses the QMS's performance.

Conclusion

Creating an **implementation plan** for ISO 9001 is a strategic process that ensures an organized, systematic, and successful adoption of a **Quality Management System**. By defining clear objectives, assigning responsibilities, allocating resources, and regularly reviewing progress, small enterprises can implement ISO 9001 effectively, paving the way for long-term success.

This plan will not only guide the organization through the complexities of ISO 9001 but also lay the foundation for continuous improvement, customer satisfaction, and operational excellence.

Allocating Resources for ISO 9001

Allocating the right **resources** is a crucial aspect of successfully implementing and maintaining **ISO 9001:2015**. The effectiveness of the **Quality Management System (QMS)** largely depends on the resources available and how well they are used to support the system. Resources refer not only to financial investments but also to human, technological, and physical resources that ensure the system's success. Proper allocation and management of these resources will directly impact the efficiency of the QMS and the organization's ability to meet customer requirements and continually improve.

In this section, we will explore how to allocate **resources** effectively for ISO 9001 implementation, covering human resources, infrastructure, financial resources, and technological support.

Key Resources Required for ISO 9001 Implementation

1. **Human Resources**
    - **Skilled Personnel**: One of the most critical resources for ISO 9001 implementation is **human resources**. This involves having employees with the right skills and expertise to design, implement, and maintain the QMS. ISO 9001 requires a **cross-functional approach**, so employees from different departments must be involved in the implementation process, including leadership, quality management, production, HR, and customer service teams.
    - **Training and Competence**: Employees must be **trained** on the requirements of ISO 9001 and their roles within the QMS. This includes understanding the processes, procedures, and responsibilities

associated with the QMS. Top management and senior leaders must ensure that all employees understand the importance of quality and their contribution to meeting customer satisfaction.

- **Quality Manager/Coordinator**: Appointing a **Quality Manager** or **Quality Coordinator** is essential for overseeing the implementation and monitoring of the QMS. This person will play a central role in managing the development of quality documentation, conducting audits, and ensuring the QMS complies with ISO 9001 standards.

Resource	Description	Importance
Skilled Personnel	Employees with knowledge of QMS processes and ISO 9001 requirements.	Ensures the effective implementation and operation of the QMS.
Training	Training employees on ISO 9001 principles, procedures, and their roles.	Equips employees with the necessary knowledge to maintain QMS effectiveness.
Quality Manager	Designating a quality manager to oversee QMS implementation.	Ensures the QMS is properly implemented and managed.

2. **Infrastructure and Physical Resources**
   - **Physical Infrastructure**: This includes facilities, buildings, equipment, machinery, and tools required to produce goods or deliver services. For ISO 9001 compliance, organizations must ensure that their infrastructure is capable of supporting **quality processes** effectively.
   - **Work Environment**: A safe, efficient, and organized work environment is essential for maintaining high-quality standards. It should be conducive to producing high-quality products or services while minimizing errors, downtime, and inefficiencies.
   - **Technology and Equipment**: The organization needs to ensure that it has the right **technology and equipment** to perform processes effectively. This includes machinery, IT systems, and software tools needed for production, quality control, and tracking performance. Technological support, such as **automated testing equipment**, **document management systems**, and **monitoring tools**, is essential for improving the efficiency and accuracy of processes.

Resource	Description	Importance
Physical Infrastructure	Buildings, equipment, and facilities necessary for production or service.	Supports the quality of products/services delivered.
Work Environment	Creating a safe and productive working environment.	Reduces errors, increases efficiency, and boosts employee morale.
Technology and Equipment	Tools and technology needed to perform processes and track quality.	Enhances process efficiency and improves quality control.

3. **Financial Resources**
    - **Budget Allocation**: The financial resources required to implement ISO 9001 include costs for documentation, training, software tools, audits, certification, and continuous improvement initiatives. Allocating sufficient **budget** is crucial to ensuring the QMS is properly developed and maintained.
    - **Cost Control and Efficiency**: Effective use of financial resources also involves **cost management**. The organization should plan and track expenditures to ensure that the QMS implementation does not exceed the allocated budget while still meeting the requirements of ISO 9001.
    - **Continuous Improvement**: ISO 9001 is centered around continual improvement, and this requires ongoing investment in process improvements, technology, and employee development. The organization must allocate funds for **periodic audits**, **corrective actions**, and **quality improvement initiatives**.

Resource	Description	Importance
Budget Allocation	Allocation of sufficient financial resources for the QMS implementation.	Ensures that the necessary funds are available for successful ISO 9001 adoption.
Cost Control	Monitoring and controlling costs during QMS implementation.	Keeps implementation within budget and ensures efficient use of resources.
Investment in Improvement	Allocating funds for continuous improvements and audits.	Ensures ongoing improvement and compliance with ISO 9001 standards.

4. **Technological Resources**
   - **Software Tools**: Effective QMS implementation often involves adopting software tools that help manage quality processes. This could include **Document Management Systems (DMS)** to manage procedures, records, and work instructions, or **Enterprise Resource Planning (ERP)** systems that help integrate different business functions (e.g., HR, finance, production) with the QMS.
   - **Monitoring Tools**: Technology is also needed to monitor key performance indicators (KPIs), track nonconformities, measure customer satisfaction, and evaluate supplier performance. Software tools can assist in **data collection**, **analysis**, and **reporting** for better decision-making.
   - **Communication Systems**: Effective communication is vital for the success of the QMS. **Collaborative platforms** (e.g., intranet, email systems, project management tools) help ensure that information regarding quality policies, objectives, and improvements is shared efficiently across the organization.

Resource	Description	Importance
Software Tools	Tools for document management, ERP, and quality management.	Improves efficiency, reduces errors, and supports accurate tracking.
Monitoring Tools	Tools for tracking KPIs, nonconformities, and performance.	Helps monitor the effectiveness of the QMS and supports continuous improvement.
Communication Systems	Tools to facilitate communication across the organization.	Ensures that information is shared effectively and timely.

Benefits of Proper Resource Allocation for ISO 9001

Proper allocation of resources is integral to the success of the QMS. Here are some of the benefits:

Benefit	Description

Increased Efficiency	Effective resource allocation improves process efficiency and reduces downtime.
Higher Product Quality	Adequate resources ensure that processes run smoothly, resulting in higher-quality products and services.
Employee Satisfaction	Proper training, the right tools, and an effective work environment improve employee morale and engagement.
Cost Savings	Properly managing resources can reduce waste, lower costs, and improve profitability.
Continual Improvement	Sufficient resources for training and monitoring support ongoing process improvements.

Conclusion

Allocating **resources for ISO 9001** implementation is not only about ensuring sufficient budget, technology, and infrastructure but also about **empowering people**. The right investment in **human resources**, **training**, **technology**, and **processes** will enable an organization to effectively implement and maintain the QMS, achieve certification, and sustain continual improvement. Ensuring that these resources are used effectively supports the organization's long-term **success**, **customer satisfaction**, and **compliance** with the ISO 9001 standards.

Managing Time and Budget Constraints in ISO 9001 Implementation

Successfully implementing **ISO 9001:2015** requires careful management of both **time** and **budget**. These two constraints often present significant challenges, particularly for small enterprises with limited resources. However, by planning ahead and following structured approaches, organizations can overcome these challenges, ensuring that the **Quality Management System (QMS)** is implemented efficiently and within budget.

This section will explore how to effectively manage **time** and **budget** during the ISO 9001 implementation process, ensuring that the project remains on track, meets deadlines, and stays within financial constraints, all while achieving the desired quality standards.

Key Considerations for Managing Time and Budget

1. Developing a Realistic Timeline

A well-structured **timeline** is essential for managing the time aspect of ISO 9001 implementation. Without a clear timeline, the project may experience delays, cost overruns, and confusion regarding milestones and deadlines.

Key Steps in Developing a Timeline:

- **Define Phases of Implementation**: Break the implementation into clear phases, such as **planning**, **training**, **documentation**, **internal audits**, and **management review**.
- **Set Milestones**: Establish **milestones** within each phase to track progress. For instance, completing the gap analysis, developing the quality policy, or holding the first internal audit can be defined as milestones.
- **Allocate Time for Each Task**: Assign specific timeframes to each task or milestone. It is important to balance speed with quality, ensuring that tasks are not rushed but also do not overrun.
- **Adjust for Contingencies**: Include some buffer time for unexpected challenges. Having some extra time allocated for unforeseen issues will help prevent the project from falling behind.

Action	Description
Define Implementation Phases	Break down the ISO 9001 implementation into manageable phases.
Set Milestones	Identify key milestones to track progress effectively.
Allocate Time for Tasks	Assign realistic timeframes to each task to ensure timely completion.
Include Buffer Time	Account for contingencies and potential setbacks.

2. Prioritizing Key Activities

While it's important to develop a comprehensive plan, it is equally crucial to **prioritize key activities** that are essential to the QMS's success. Some tasks may be more time-sensitive or critical to achieving certification, so focusing on those first can help streamline the process.

How to Prioritize:

- **Focus on Critical Tasks**: Identify tasks that must be completed first, such as **defining the scope**, **establishing quality objectives**, or **developing key documentation**.
- **Identify Bottlenecks**: Look for potential bottlenecks, such as **resource shortages** or **complex tasks** that may take more time and effort to complete. Address these issues early.
- **Use the 80/20 Rule**: Prioritize the **20% of tasks** that will yield **80% of the benefits**. For example, aligning processes to meet customer requirements may have a significant impact on the overall quality of the system.

Action	Description
Prioritize Critical Tasks	Focus on high-impact tasks that are essential for certification.
Identify Bottlenecks	Recognize potential delays and address them in advance.
Use the 80/20 Rule	Focus on tasks that deliver the most significant benefits.

3. Monitoring Progress and Tracking Time

Regular monitoring of **progress** is essential to ensure that the implementation stays on schedule. By **tracking time** spent on various tasks, organizations can identify delays early and take corrective action before they escalate.

Steps to Monitor Time and Progress:

- **Use Project Management Tools**: Tools like Gantt charts, task lists, or project management software (e.g., Trello, Asana) can help track tasks and deadlines.
- **Regular Reviews**: Schedule periodic reviews (e.g., weekly or bi-weekly) to assess progress, address any challenges, and adjust the timeline as necessary.
- **Maintain Communication**: Ensure that the project team and management are kept informed of progress. Regular communication helps identify issues early and makes it easier to resolve them promptly.

Action	Description
Use Project Management Tools	Leverage tools for better tracking and visualization of tasks.
Regular Reviews	Conduct periodic check-ins to track progress against the timeline.
Maintain Communication	Ensure ongoing communication among the project team and management.

4. Managing the Budget and Costs

The financial aspect of ISO 9001 implementation can be challenging, especially for small enterprises with limited resources. Proper budgeting, tracking expenses, and cost management are crucial to ensure that the implementation remains financially viable.

Key Steps in Managing the Budget:

- **Estimate Costs for Each Task**: Break down the budget by task or phase, estimating the costs associated with each activity, such as **training**, **documentation**, **audits**, **certification fees**, and **consultants**.
- **Track Expenditures**: Continuously monitor expenses to ensure that they align with the budget. This helps avoid cost overruns and enables proactive action if costs exceed expectations.
- **Control Unnecessary Expenses**: Identify areas where costs can be reduced without compromising the quality of the implementation, such as limiting external consultations or using in-house resources for training.
- **Reallocate Funds if Necessary**: If unforeseen expenses arise, reallocate funds from less critical tasks to ensure key activities are well-funded.

Action	Description
Estimate Task Costs	Break down the budget for each phase or task to track expenses.
Track Expenditures	Monitor expenses regularly to stay within the allocated budget.
Control Unnecessary Costs	Identify and eliminate any unnecessary expenses.
Reallocate Funds	Adjust the budget allocation as necessary to meet critical needs.

5. Contingency Planning for Unexpected Costs

Even with careful planning, unexpected challenges and costs may arise during the implementation of ISO 9001. It is essential to include a **contingency plan** to address these uncertainties and ensure the project can continue smoothly without significant financial setbacks.

How to Plan for Contingencies:

- **Set Aside a Contingency Fund**: Allocate a portion of the budget (typically 5-10%) as a contingency fund for unforeseen expenses.

- **Anticipate Common Issues**: Identify potential problems in advance (e.g., training delays, extended audit timelines, equipment failure) and plan resources accordingly.
- **Monitor Contingency Usage**: Track how contingency funds are used, ensuring that they are only allocated to address legitimate, unexpected issues.

Action	Description
Set Aside a Contingency Fund	Allocate funds to cover unforeseen issues.
Anticipate Common Issues	Identify potential problems early to minimize disruptions.
Monitor Contingency Usage	Track how contingency funds are used to stay within budget.

Benefits of Effective Time and Budget Management

Proper management of **time** and **budget** during ISO 9001 implementation has several significant benefits:

Benefit	Description
Efficiency	Proper time and budget management ensures that the QMS is implemented efficiently without delays or unnecessary expenses.
Cost Savings	Effective budget control helps minimize costs, reducing the overall expenditure of implementing ISO 9001.
On-Time Completion	A well-managed timeline ensures that the QMS is implemented on time, leading to timely certification and operational improvements.
Sustainable Results	Managing resources ensures that the QMS is not only implemented effectively but also maintained and improved over time.
Reduced Risk of Non-Compliance	Staying on track with the timeline and budget reduces the risk of delays that could affect ISO 9001 certification.

Conclusion

Managing time and budget constraints during **ISO 9001 implementation** is critical to the success of the QMS. By developing a realistic timeline, prioritizing key tasks, tracking progress, managing financial resources, and planning for contingencies, organizations can ensure that the QMS is implemented efficiently, within budget, and on time. Effective time and budget management ultimately supports the achievement of ISO 9001 certification and enables the organization to benefit from improved quality, customer satisfaction, and operational efficiency.

Managing Time and Budget Constraints: Further Insights

Managing **time** and **budget** constraints throughout the ISO 9001 implementation process is crucial not only for the smooth implementation of the **Quality Management System (QMS)** but also for the long-term sustainability of the organization. By ensuring that the QMS implementation is both **time-efficient** and **cost-effective**, organizations can maximize the benefits of ISO 9001 certification while avoiding unnecessary disruptions or financial strain.

After setting a realistic timeline, allocating resources, and tracking expenses, there are several more considerations that can enhance **time** and **budget management** during ISO 9001 implementation. These additional insights help ensure that the organization remains agile and prepared for unforeseen challenges during the process.

6. Efficient Use of External Expertise

For many organizations, especially small enterprises with limited in-house expertise, bringing in **external consultants** or **specialists** may be essential for the implementation of ISO 9001. However, hiring external consultants can quickly become a significant portion of the **budget**. Therefore, it's important to use external expertise efficiently.

Steps to Efficiently Use External Expertise:

- **Define Clear Roles for Consultants**: Clearly define the scope and responsibilities of external consultants to ensure that their efforts are focused on areas where the organization lacks expertise, such as documentation creation, gap analysis, or training.
- **Use Consultants for Critical Tasks**: Limit the use of consultants to key areas where in-house expertise is insufficient. For example, a consultant can guide the organization through the initial **gap analysis** and help develop **quality policies** but can leave the more straightforward tasks to internal teams.
- **Ensure Knowledge Transfer**: Consultants should not only perform tasks but also train the internal team, transferring knowledge that can reduce future reliance on external support. This will help manage costs while building internal capabilities for ongoing QMS maintenance.

Benefits:

- **Cost Control**: Using consultants only for essential tasks minimizes the financial burden.
- **Knowledge Transfer**: Internal teams can become self-sufficient after the consultant's involvement, ensuring the long-term success of the QMS.

7. Managing Resource Allocation Throughout the Implementation

A key challenge in managing both time and budget is ensuring that **resources are allocated efficiently** throughout the various stages of ISO 9001 implementation. Efficient resource allocation helps prevent the overuse of time or budget at any single stage, ensuring that the organization remains within its limits.

Steps for Efficient Resource Allocation:

- **Balanced Resource Distribution**: Allocate resources proportionally to each stage of the implementation process. For instance, initial stages such as **training** and **documentation development** may require more time and financial resources, while later stages, such as **internal audits** or **management reviews**, may need less financial input but more human resources.
- **Avoid Over-Allocation**: Avoid over-allocating resources to non-critical areas. Focus on areas with the highest impact on achieving certification and quality objectives.
- **Monitor Resource Usage Regularly**: Keep track of how resources are used throughout the process. This helps identify any imbalances or inefficiencies early, allowing for adjustments as needed.

Benefits:

- **Prevents Over-expenditure**: Ensures that resources are used where they will have the greatest impact, avoiding wasted efforts and costs.
- **Maximizes Efficiency**: Helps organizations stay on track without overburdening their resources at any stage of the implementation.

8. Post-Implementation Monitoring and Adjustment

Once the ISO 9001 QMS has been implemented and the certification process is complete, it's important to continue managing time and budget through the **post-implementation phase**. This phase focuses on maintaining the QMS, ensuring its **continuous improvement**, and periodically reviewing whether the processes remain aligned with ISO 9001 standards.

Steps for Post-Implementation Monitoring:

- **Conduct Regular Audits**: Perform regular internal audits to ensure that the QMS remains compliant with ISO 9001 standards. These audits help identify areas for improvement and ensure that the system continues to function efficiently.
- **Review QMS Performance**: Periodically review the performance of the QMS against the **quality objectives** and **KPIs** set during the planning phase. Ensure that the system is delivering the expected results and meeting customer requirements.
- **Adjust Resources as Needed**: As the QMS matures, the resource needs may change. For instance, if a process becomes more efficient or if new technology is implemented, the allocation of resources may need to be adjusted to reflect the new needs.
- **Allocate Budget for Ongoing Improvements**: Ensure that a portion of the budget is set aside for continuous improvement initiatives. ISO 9001 is based on a model of continual improvement, so regular investments in training, technology, and process enhancements are necessary.

Benefits:

- **Continuous Improvement**: Ensures that the QMS remains relevant, effective, and aligned with the organization's goals.
- **Cost Efficiency**: Regular monitoring helps identify areas where resources can be better allocated to improve efficiency and reduce costs.
- **Sustained Success**: Post-implementation adjustments ensure that the organization maintains ISO 9001 standards and achieves long-term success.

9. Use of Lean and Agile Approaches to Streamline the Process

Incorporating **lean** and **agile principles** into the QMS implementation process can help streamline the process, reduce waste, and ensure that the implementation stays within the set time and budget constraints.

Key Lean and Agile Approaches:

- **Focus on Value**: Prioritize activities that add the most value to the organization, such as **customer satisfaction** and **process efficiency**. Eliminate or minimize activities that do not contribute significantly to the QMS objectives.
- **Iterative Implementation**: Rather than trying to implement the entire QMS in one go, use an **iterative approach** to gradually roll out different aspects of the QMS. This allows the organization to assess the effectiveness of each stage and make adjustments as necessary.
- **Flexible Resource Allocation**: Be prepared to adapt resources as needed. If one phase requires more time or financial input than initially expected, reallocate resources from less critical areas.

Conclusion

Effectively managing **time** and **budget** constraints during ISO 9001 implementation is critical for success. By developing a realistic timeline, prioritizing key tasks, monitoring progress regularly, allocating resources efficiently, and planning for contingencies, organizations can ensure that the QMS implementation process is smooth, on time, and within budget. Additionally, **post-implementation reviews**, **continuous monitoring**, and the use of **lean and agile approaches** ensure the ongoing success and sustainability of the QMS.

With these strategies in place, an organization can not only achieve ISO 9001 certification but also establish a strong foundation for **continual improvement**, **customer satisfaction**, and **operational excellence**.

Congratulations on completing the guide to ISO 9001 for Small Enterprises!

We hope this book has equipped you with the knowledge and tools to successfully implement a **Quality Management System (QMS)** in your organization. Achieving ISO 9001 certification is an important milestone that enhances quality, operational efficiency, and customer satisfaction.

As you move forward with your QMS journey, remember that it's about continuous improvement and a commitment to quality. Use this guide as a reference to ensure your system remains effective and aligned with your business goals.

Best of luck in your journey towards ISO 9001 certification, and may it lead to greater success for your organization!

www.ingramcontent.com/pod-product-compliance
Lightning Source LLC
Chambersburg PA
CBHW041748220926
51847CB00013B/145
* 9 7 8 3 8 5 2 2 8 1 5 7 5 *